CHRISTIAN PUBLISHING
HOUSE & PROBE MINISTRIES

ARTS, MEDIA, AND CULTURE

A Biblical Point of View

KERBY ANDERSON

All things are permitted for me, but not all things are profitable. All things are permitted for me, but I will not be controlled by anything.—1 Cor. 6:12.

i

ARTS, MEDIA, AND CULTURE

A Biblical Point of View

Kerby Anderson

General Editor

Christian Publishing House

Cambridge, Ohio

CPH Since 2005

Christian Publishing House

Professional Conservative Christian
Publishing of the Good News!

ARTS, MEDIA, AND CULTURE: A Biblical Point of View by Kerby Anderson

ISBN-13: 978-1-945757-30-3

ISBN-10: 1-945757-30-2

Table of Contents

What is art? How should a Christian evaluate the arts? What does the Bible say about art and

vi

Contributors

Kerby Anderson is president of Probe Ministries International. He holds masters degrees from Yale University (science) and from Georgetown University (government). He is the host of "Point of View" (USA Radio Network) heard on 300+ radio outlets nationwide as well as on the Internet (www.pointofview.net) and shortwave. He is also a regular guest on "Prime Time America" (Moody Broadcasting Network) and "Fire Away" (American Family Radio).

Jerry Solomon, former Director of Field Ministries and Mind Games Coordinator for Probe Ministries, served as Associate Pastor at Dallas Bible Church after leaving Probe. He received the B.A. in Bible and the M.A. in history and theology from Criswell College. He also attended the University of North Texas, Canal Zone College, and Lebanon Valley College.

Todd Kappelman is a field associate with Probe Ministries. He is a graduate of Dallas Baptist University (B.A. and M.A.B.S., religion and Greek), and the University of Dallas (M.A., philosophy/humanities). Currently he is pursuing a Ph.D. in philosophy at the University of Dallas. He has served as assistant director of the Trinity Institute, a study center devoted to Christian thought and inquiry.

James Williams is the founder and past president of Probe Ministries International. He holds degrees from Southern Methodist University (B.A.) and Dallas Theological Seminary (Th.M.). He also has pursued inter-disciplinary doctoral studies in the humanities at the University of Texas at Dallas.

Sarah Withers served as an intern with Probe Ministries. She is a student at Covenant College, majoring in Philosophy and History. She serves as an editor for Mountaintop Thoughts, the college's philosophy journal. When she's not leading others as a Resident Assistant, Sarah enjoys playing with her dog Ginger and being outdoors.

Preface

Our culture is filled with a variety of worldviews, each competing for our attention and allegiance. How should we as Christians relate to the culture? How can we make sense of these worldviews? Should Christians embrace the arts or reject them? How can we apply biblical principles of discernment to the arts and media?

These are significant questions that deserve thoughtful answers. The following chapters provide a "road map" which can be used to understand and evaluate various worldviews and how they are expressed in the arts and media. The Bible teaches that as Christian disciples, we should not be conformed to this world (Romans 12:2). Instead, we are to transform our minds through the renewing power of Christ. Hopefully, this book will enable you to do so.

The following chapters first aired as Probe radio programs, and many of them were collected in the earlier book: *Arts, Entertainment & Christian Values* (Grand Rapids, MI: Kregel, 2000). Jerry Solomon (who is no longer living) wrote many of these chapters, and we wanted to make them available once again to a new generation of believers who need to know how to analyze culture and the arts.

The first section examines the relationship Christians should have with the culture and then provides an overview of worldviews as well an historic look at worldviews through history. The second and third sections discuss how Christians can evaluate various forms of art and media.

Read through these chapters and consider how you will be the salt of the earth and the light of the world (Matthew 5:13-16). Then go and live out your Christian faith before the watching world.

SECTION 1 CULTURE

How should a Christian relate to culture? Are we merely to be separate from the world or is there a place for Christians to transform culture? What are the major worldviews in society? How can we evaluate these various worldviews?

CHAPTER 1 Christians and Culture

Jerry Solomon

What do you think of when you hear the word culture? Perhaps you refer to the arts. You may picture the way people dress, the way they eat, their language, their religion, their architecture, or a host of other perceptions. One of the most succinct definitions of culture is wide-ranging because it refers to "that which man does beyond biological necessity."[1] Obviously such a definition indicates the importance of the term. Our lives are lived within culture. There is no escaping this thing called culture. But how is a Christian to respond?

Church history demonstrates that one of the constant struggles of Christianity, both individually and corporately, is with culture. Paul, for example, wrote two letters to Christians who lived in Corinth, a very challenging culture. Where should we stand? Inside? Outside? Ignore it? Become isolated from it? Should we concern ourselves with attempting to transform it?

Paradigms of Culture

In 1949, a theologian named Richard Niebuhr delivered a series of lectures entitled *Christ and Culture*.[2] Subsequently his thoughts were published and the book has become a classic. Niebuhr's text focuses on five paradigms that describe how Christians have dealt with

---

[1] Emil Brunner, *Christianity and Civilization* (London: Nisbet, 1948), 142.

[2] H. Richard Niebuhr, *Christ and Culture* (New York: Harper & Row, 1951).

culture. A brief survey of these paradigms can help us see ourselves, and perhaps challenge us to consider changing the way we look at the world around us.

The first paradigm, *Christ against Culture*, describes those who choose to isolate themselves from the surrounding culture. A descriptive contemporary phrase might be "the holy huddle" of Christians who dialog among themselves, but no one else. Second, the *Christ of Culture* perspective is exactly the opposite of *Christ against Culture* because it attempts to bring culture and Christianity together, regardless of their differences. Third, the *Christ above Culture* position attempts to synthesize the issues of the culture with the answer of Christian revelation. Fourth, *Christ and Culture in Paradox* refers to those who understand the tension between the Christian's responsibility to both the cultural and the spiritual realms. Fifth, *Christ the Transformer of Culture* describes those who strive "to convert the values and goals of secular culture into the service of the kingdom of God."[3]

Which of these paradigms describes your relationship with the culture in which you live? Or perhaps you have another paradigm to offer. No doubt we could engage in debate about the merits and demerits of all of them. But since we cannot do that at the moment, let us agree that we should at least give attention to our place in culture.

Christians are to observe and analyze culture and make decisions regarding our proper actions and reactions within it. A struggle is in progress and the stakes are high. But in order to struggle meaningfully and with some hope of influencing our culture, we must be thoughtful and informed.

---

[3] Donald G. Bloesch, *Freedom for Obedience* (San Francisco: Harpter & Row, 1987), 227.

Our work through Probe Ministries is dedicated to the proposition that the Lord can use Christians as salt and light. God has called us to offer a voice in both the Christian and the non- Christian communities. Among other things, this means that we have attempted to give attention to how this can be done for the glory of God. In particular, our involvement in the non-Christian community presents a special challenge. Much prayer and study have been focused on principles that should be considered before we engage with the culture. In this article, I will focus on five of these principles that apply to ministry within the culture.

Establishing Biblical Precepts

Unless you live in a cave, you have had to deal with the culture around you. You have sensed the need to give thought to how you might glorify God as you react to your culture. Or you may have experienced times of mental and spiritual trauma as you realized the sinful nature of what you experience around you. If you choose to interact with your culture, there are certain principles to be considered.

The first of these is the need for biblical precepts. That is, our minds should be filled with God's ideas before interacting with the culture. This is an understandable and universally stated declaration among evangelical Christians. Experience tells us we need to give life to the declaration. Are we responding to our culture based on biblical precepts, or are we responding to our culture based on other sources? Are we utilizing a Christian world view as we respond to culture, or are we unwittingly utilizing a naturalistic worldview? When we discuss things as Christians, do we focus on Scripture no matter what we might be discussing? "Contemporary Christianity is all too frequently shaped by the fact that when we meet we do so in an atmosphere resembling that of a committee or caucus, where the style is political and tactical, hardly scholarly, and almost never devotional or genuinely spiritual."[4] Do we give serious attention "to the sacred text as the firm and only basis on which life and decisions should be based?"[5] Indeed, without the "sacred text" evangelicals are left to grapple with their culture in much the same manner as those who do not claim allegiance to that text.

In order to affirm the primacy of Scripture in a cultural critique the Christian should first *read* his culture in the light of the Bible. Proper recognition of the culture is necessary before it can be addressed properly. In other words, we need a biblical "lens" through which we can see the culture. The light of God's Word needs to be focused on the questions at hand. For example, the culture tends to *secularize* life. Most of us live, work, and play in the secular sphere. But *secularism* refers to a way of life that "excludes all considerations drawn from a belief in God or in a future state."[6]

Harry Blamires, a protégé of C.S. Lewis and an astute cultural critic, offers an insightful critique of secularism.

> The secularist's position can be defined only in negatives. There is no life except this life in time. There is no order of being except that which we explore with our senses and our instruments. There is no condition of well-being except that of a healthy and comfortable life in time. There is no God to be worshipped, for no God created us. There is no God to propitiate,

---

[4] Charles E. Kinzie, "The Absorbed Church: Our Inheritance of Conformed Christianity," *Sojourners* 7 (July, 1978), 22.

[5] Ibid.

[6] Harry Blamires, *The Christian Mind* (Ann Arbor, MI: Servant, 1963), 58.

7

for there is no God to offend. There is no reward to be sought and no punishment to be avoided except those which derive from earthly authority. There is no law to be obeyed except those which earthly authority imposes or earthly prudence recommends.[7]

Obviously, Blamires' observations are the result of seeing secularism with a scriptural lens. Biblical precepts allow him to offer such a critique. His example can be an encouragement for us. May God guide us as we apply biblical precepts to evaluate our culture.

Rejecting Cultural Biases, Developing Interaction

What do you think of the culture in which you live? In particular, what do you think of the broader American culture in which your sub-culture is found? For example, are you comfortable with the adage: "America: love it or leave it?" Or do you tend to think of certain other cultures as pristine, even if you have never visited them?

I have discussed the need to assess culture through the use of biblical precepts, the first principle of cultural evaluation. The second principle is focused on what I call cultural bias. If we are to interact with cultures other than our own, and if we seek honestly to evaluate our own, we must be cautious of biases.

Carl F.H. Henry, a great theologian, apologist, and cultural critic has enumerated what he calls twenty fantasies of a secular society. One of these includes the thought that God "will protect the United States and its people from catastrophic disaster because of our commitment to freedom, generosity, and goodness." Dr.

---

[7] Harry Blamires, *Recovering the Christian Mind* (Downers Grove, IL: InterVarsity, 1988), 59-60.

Henry writes, "For many, God is an ever-living George Washington who serves invisibly as the father of our country. This vague political theology assumes that America can never drift irrecoverably beyond divine approval, and that the nation is intrinsically exempt from severe and final divine judgment." Another fantasy is "that the American people are essentially good at heart in a world whose inhabitants are more prone to evil."[8]

The anthropologist Charles Kraft responds to such thinking by writing that "much of the Christian populace has simply continued to assume that such features of our society as monogamy, democracy, our type of educational system, individualism, capitalism, the 'freedoms,' literacy, technological development, military supremacy, etc. are all products of our association with God and therefore can be pointed to as indications of the superiority of our culture over all other cultures."[9]

Missionaries who serve in cultures other than their own can speak to the danger of such fantasies. But we do not have to be foreign missionaries to experience the effects of cultural bias. The United States has become such a multicultural environment that Christians can and must understand the importance of rejecting cultural biases.

Interaction but not Accommodation

The third principle of cultural evaluation focuses on the need for interaction with culture, but not accommodation. There should be no fear in this if we are using biblical precepts, the first of our principles. But we need to be alert to the ways in which we can become enmeshed in the culture. In addition, we should be

---

[8] Carl F.H. Henry, *Christian Countermoves In A Decadent Culture* (Portland, OR: Multnomah, 1986), 32.

[9] Charles H. Kraft, "Can Anthropological Insight Assist Evangelical Theology?" *The Christian Scholar's Review* 7 (1977), 182.

accountable to one another by offering warnings when we observe such entanglement.

Without cultural interaction, evangelicals leave numerous important facets of contemporary cultural life without the light of truth they can offer. A cursory reading of post-Enlightenment history will demonstrate the progressive decrease of evangelical interaction and the subsequent lack of influence in strategic areas of culture. For example, American higher education has been guided by principles that leave Christian theism out of the picture.

It is crucial, though, that such interaction take place with a sense of accountability. The person who enters the culture without respect for the ideological dangers that reside there will prove to be foolish. The ideas, the sense of progress, and the pride of cultural accomplishment can lead us to give credit to man instead of God. May the Lord receive praise as He uses us to touch our culture!

A Positive Revolutionary Vision

The word *revolution* tends to have a negative connotation for most of us. A revolutionary most often is seen as someone who engenders rebellion and chaos. But a Christian's response to culture should include a positive revolutionary mindset. Christian thought and life should state things to culture that exhibit Christ's revolutionary vision for all people. A type of pluralism that tempts us to negate Christianity's claims and absolutes should not persuade Christians. Donald Bloesch speaks to this tension by juxtaposing what he calls prophetic religion and culture religion. He writes: "Our choice today is between a prophetic religion and a culture religion. The first is anchored in a holy God who infinitely transcends every cultural and religious form that testifies to Him. The second absolutizes the cultural or mythical garb in which

God supposedly meets us."[10] Our interaction with culture must have a prophetic voice. We must speak boldly to the culture knowing that the source of our proclamation is the sovereign God.

This means that Christians should not relegate their lives to what may be called a "Christian ghetto" or "holy huddle." Too many Christians live "a split life: they are forced to use many words and images that have a private meaning for them with which they are unable or unwilling to enrich the fund of public experience."[11] One may have a revolutionary vision and prophetic zeal, but too often it is directed toward his "ghetto" instead of the surrounding culture. To quote an old cliché: "He is preaching to the choir."

Notice how often conversations among Christians concentrate on problems presented by the surrounding culture. For example, discussion may focus on the latest outrage in the entertainment industry, or the newest bit of intrigue in Washington, or concerns about the sex education emphasized in public schools, or controversies surrounding issues of abortion, euthanasia, cloning, homosexuality, child abuse, or a host of other topics. Then notice if constructive suggestions are offered. Is attention given to the ways in which the Christian community might respond to such issues based on biblical precepts? Too often such a scenario does not include positive revolutionary cultural interaction.

Lesslie Newbigin, a perceptive cultural critic, offers two propositions regarding a Christian's revolutionary vision. First, Newbigin states he would not see Christians just "in that corner of the private sector which our culture

---

[10] Bloesch, *Freedom for Obedience*, 244.

[11] Julius Lipner, "Being One, Let Me Be Many: Facets of the Relationship Between the Gospel and Culture," *International Review of Missions* 74 (April, 1985), 162.

labels 'religion', but rather in the public sector where God's will as declared in Jesus Christ is either done or not done in the daily business of nations and societies, in the councils of governments, the boardrooms of transnational corporations, the trade unions, the universities, and the schools." Second, "I would place the recovery of that apocalyptic strand of the New Testament teaching without which Christian hope becomes merely hope for the survival of the individual and there is no hope for the world."[12] Christianity is not to be privatized; it applies to all people in all places at all times.

If we choose to take Newbigin's propositions seriously, we must not be naïve about the response we will receive. At this moment in American history the public sector often is antagonistic toward a Christian voice. Thus we should not be surprised when we are rejected. Instead, if we are stating God's ideas we should rejoice, as did the early Christians when they suffered for His name (Acts 5:41). When truth rubs shoulders with untruth, friction is the result.

Glorifying God in All of Life

The words *whatever* and *all* are enormous. Can you think of something more than *whatever* or *all*? When the apostle Paul wrote his first letter to the church in Corinth he used these terms to describe how they should glorify God in their lives: "Whether, then, you eat or drink, or whatever you do, do all to the glory of God" (1 Cor. 10:31). Pagan Corinth certainly provided many opportunities for early Christians to learn how to respond to their culture. The same is true for Christians in our time. We live in and associate with a culture that

_____

[12] Lesslie Newbigin, "Can the West be Converted?" *Evangelical Review of Theology* 11 (October, 1987), 366.

constantly presents challenges. We are to glorify God in all we do, regardless of those challenges. "Where God is acknowledged as the Creator, man knows that the ultimate meaning of His creatures is the same as the meaning of all life: the glory of God and the service of men."[13] Our work within culture and our influence on it are part of what God will judge. Therefore, these works are important.

We are to remind ourselves and tell the culture that "the prophetic church witnesses to the breaking into history of a higher righteousness; it points people to a higher law."[14] Carl F.H. Henry emphasizes this in a passage concerning education, but the implications cover much more:

The drift of twentieth century learning can be succinctly summarized in one statement: Instead of recognizing [God] as the source and stipulator of truth and the good, contemporary thought reduces all reality to impersonal processes and events, and insists that man himself creatively imposes upon the cosmos and upon history the only values that they will ever bear.[15]

God is sovereign; He is the Lord of *whatever* and *all* in all of life. Thus we must be cautious about our emphases within culture. God changes things; we are His messengers. Our involvement is important, but it must be remembered that it is transitory. As beautiful and meaningful as the works of man may be, they will not last. The theologian Karl Barth emphasized this by relating his comments to the tower of Babel: "In the building of the tower of Babel whose top

---

[13] Emil Brunner, *Christianity and Civilization* (London: Nisbet & Co., 1948), 157.

[14] Donald Bloesch, "The Legacy of Karl Barth," *TSF Bulletin* 9 (May-June 1986), 8.

[15] Carl F.H. Henry, "The Crisis of Modern Learning," *Faculty Dialogue* 10 (Winter 1988), 7.

is to touch heaven, the Church can have no part. The hope of the Church rests *on* God *for* men; it does not rest *on* men, not even on religious men—and not even on the belief that men *with the help of God* will finally build that tower."[16] Our hope is not found in man's efforts. Our hope is found in God's provision for eternity. But this does not denigrate our involvement with culture. "There is a radical difference between human culture generally, which is thoroughly secular, and that which is developed as a loving service to God."[17] Utopia will never refer to this life. Since no culture "this side of the Parousia [Second Coming] can be recognized as divine we are limited to the more modest hope that life on earth may gradually be made better; or, more modestly still, gradually be made less bad."[18] Christian's response to culture should be described with such modest hopes in view.

This article has focused on five principles that can strengthen a Christian impact on culture. Fill your mind with biblical precepts; be careful that you do not respond to the surrounding culture with cultural biases; be interactive, but not accommodating; develop a positive revolutionary mindset; and glorify God in all of life.

---

[16] Karl Barth, *Theology and Church*, trans. Louise Pettibone Smith (New York: Harper & Row, 1962), 349.

[17] Joseph A. Hill, "Human Culture in Biblical Perspective," *Presbyterian Journal*, 18 February 1981, 9.

[18] Stephen Mayor, "Jesus Christ and the Christian Understanding of Society," *Scottish Journal of Theology* 32 (1979), 59-60.

CHAPTER 2 Christianity and Culture

Jerry Solomon

American evangelicals find themselves in a diverse, pluralistic culture. Many ideas vie for attention and allegiance. These ideas, philosophies, or worldviews are the products of philosophical and cultural changes.

Such changes have come to define our culture. For example, pluralism can mean that all worldviews are correct and that it is intolerable to state otherwise; secularism reigns; absolutes have ceased to exist; facts can only be stated in the realm of science, not religion; evangelical Christianity has become nothing more than a troublesome oddity amidst diversity. It is clear, therefore, that western culture is suffering; it is ill. Lesslie Newbigin, a scholar and former missionary to India, has emphasized this by asking a provocative question: "Can the West be converted?"[19]

Such a question leads us to another: How is a Christian supposed to respond to such conditions? Or, how should we deal with the culture that surrounds us?

Since the term *culture* is central in this discussion, it deserves particular attention and definition. Even though the concept behind the word is ancient, and it is used frequently in many different contexts, its actual meaning is elusive and often confusing. *Culture* does not refer to a particular level of life. This level, sometimes referred to as "high culture," is certainly an integral part of the definition, but it is not the central focus. For example,

---

[19] Lesslie Newbigin, "Can the West be Converted?" *Evangelical Review of Theology* 11 (October 1987).

"the arts" are frequently identified with culture in the minds of many. More often than not there is a qualitative difference between what is a part of "high culture" and other segments of culture, but these distinctions are not our concern at this time.

T. S. Eliot has written that culture "may . . . be described simply as that which makes life worth living."[20] Emil Brunner, a theologian, has stated: "that culture is materialisation of meaning."[21] Donald Bloesch, another theologian, says that culture "is the task appointed to humans to realize their destiny in the world in service to the glory of God."[22] An anthropologist, E. Adamson Hoebel, believes that culture "is the integrated system of learned behavior patterns which are characteristic of the members of a society and which are not the result of biological inheritance."[23] All of these definitions can be combined to include the world views, actions, and products of a given community of people.

Christians are to observe and analyze culture and make decisions regarding our proper actions and reactions within it. A struggle is in progress and the stakes are high. Harry Blamires writes: "No thoughtful Christian can contemplate and analyze the tensions all about us in both public and private life without sensing the eternal momentousness of the current struggle for the human

---

[20] T. S. Eliot, *Christianity and Culture* (New York: Harcourt, Brace & World, 1949), 100.

[21] Emil Brunner, *Christianity and Civilization* (London: Nisbet, 1948), 62.

[22] Donald G. Bloesch, *Freedom for Obedience* (San Francisco: Harper & Row, 1987), 54.

[23] E. Adamson Hoebel, *Anthropology: The Study of Man*, 3d ed. (New York: McGraw-Hill, 1966), 5.

mind between Christian teaching and materialistic secularism."[24]

Believers are called to join the struggle. But in order to struggle meaningfully and with some hope of influencing our culture, we must be informed and thoughtful Christians. There is no room for sloth or apathy. Rev. 3:15-16 states, "I know your deeds, that you are neither cold nor hot; I would that you were cold or hot. So because you are lukewarm, and neither hot nor cold, I spit you out of my mouth."

God forbid that these words of condemnation should apply to us.

Transforming Culture

Church history demonstrates that one of the constant struggles of Christianity, both individually and corporately, is with culture. Where should we stand? Inside the culture? Outside? Ignore it? Isolate ourselves from it? Should we try to transform it?

The theologian Richard Niebuhr provided a classic study concerning these questions in his book *Christ and Culture*. Even though his theology is not always evangelical, his paradigm is helpful. It includes five views.

First, he describes the "Christ Against Culture" view, which encourages opposition, total separation, and hostility toward culture. Tertullian, Tolstoy, Menno Simons, and, in our day, Jacques Ellul are exponents of this position.

Second, the "Christ of Culture" perspective is exactly the opposite of "Christ Against Culture" because it attempts to bring culture and Christianity together,

---

[24] Harry Blamires, *Recovering the Christian Mind* (Downers Grove, Ill.: InterVarsity, 1988), 10.

regardless of their differences. Liberation, process, and feminist theologies are current examples.

Third, the "Christ Above Culture" position attempts "to correlate the fundamental questions of the culture with the answer of Christian revelation."[25] Thomas Aquinas is the most prominent teacher of this view.

Fourth, "Christ and Culture in Paradox" describes the "dualists" who stress that the Christian belongs "to two realms (the spiritual and temporal) and must live in the tension of fulfilling responsibilities to both."[26] Luther adopted this view.

Fifth, "Christ the Transformer of Culture" includes the "conversionists" who attempt "to convert the values and goals of secular culture into the service of the kingdom of God."[27] Augustine, Calvin, John Wesley, and Jonathan Edwards are the chief proponents of this last view.

With the understanding that we are utilizing a tool and not a perfected system, I believe that the "Christ the Transformer of Culture" view aligns most closely with Scripture. We are to be actively involved in the transformation of culture without giving that culture undue prominence. As the social critic Herbert Schlossberg says, "The 'salt' of people changed by the gospel must change the world."[28] Admittedly, such a perspective calls for an alertness and sensitivity to subtle dangers. But the effort is needed to follow the biblical pattern.

If we are to be transformers, we must also be "discerners," a very important word for contemporary

---

[25] Bloesch, *Freedom*, 227.

[26] Ibid.

[27] Ibid.

[28] Herbert Schlossberg, *Idols for Destruction* (Nashville, Tenn.: Thomas Nelson, 1983), 324.

18

Christians. We are to apply "the faculty of discerning; discrimination; acuteness of judgment and understanding."[29] Matthew 16:3 includes a penetrating question from Jesus to the Pharisees and Sadducees who were testing Him by asking for a sign from heaven: "Do you know how to discern the appearance of the sky, but cannot *discern* the signs of the times?" It is obvious that Jesus was disheartened by their lack of discernment. If they were alert, they could see that the Lord was demonstrating and would demonstrate (in v. 4 He refers to impending resurrection) His claims. Jesus' question is still relevant. We too must be alert and able to discern our times.

In order to transform the culture, we must continually recognize what is in need of transformation and what is not. This is a difficult assignment. We cannot afford to approach the responsibility without the guidance of God's Spirit, Word, wisdom, and power. As the theologian John Baille has said, "In proportion as a society relaxes its hold upon the eternal, it ensures the corruption of the temporal."[30] May we live in our temporal setting with a firm grasp of God's eternal claims while we transform the culture he has entrusted to us!

Stewardship and Creativity

An important aspect of our discussion of Christians and culture is centered in the early passages of the Bible.

The first two chapters of Genesis provide a foundation for God's view of culture and man's responsibility in it. These chapters contain what is generally called the "cultural mandate," God's

---

[29] *The Random House Dictionary of the English Language*, s.v. "discernment."

[30] John Baille, *What is Christian Civilization?* (London: Oxford, 1945), 59.

instructions concerning the care of His creation. Included in this are the concepts of "stewardship" and "creativity."

The mandate of stewardship is specifically found within 1:27-28 and 2:15, even though these two chapters as a whole also demonstrate it. Verse 28 of chapter 1 reads, "And God blessed them; and God said to them, "Be fruitful and multiply, and fill the earth, and subdue it; and rule over the fish of the sea and over the birds of the sky, and over every living thing that moves on the earth."

This verse contains the word *subdue*, an expression that is helpful in determining the mandate of stewardship. First, it should be observed that man is created "in the image of God." Volumes have been written about the meaning of this phrase.

Obviously, it is a very positive statement. If man is created in God's image, that image must contain God's benevolent goodness, and not maliciousness. Second, it is obvious that God's created order includes industriousness, work–a striving on the part of man. Thus we are to exercise our minds and bodies in service to God by "subduing," observing, touching, and molding the "stuff" of creation. We are to form a culture.

Tragically, because of sin, man abused his stewardship. We are now in a struggle that was not originally intended. But the redeemed person, the person in Christ, is refashioned. He can now approach culture with a clearer understanding of God's mandate. He can now begin again to exercise proper stewardship.

The mandate concerning creativity is broadly implied within the first two chapters of Genesis. It is not an emphatic pronouncement, as is the mandate concerning stewardship. In reality, the term is a misnomer, for we cannot *create* anything. We can only redesign, rearrange, or refashion what God has created.

But in this discussion we will continue to use the word with this understanding in mind.

A return to the opening chapter of Genesis leads us to an intriguing question. Of what does the "image of God" consist? It is interesting to note, as did the British writer Dorothy Sayers, that if one stops with the first chapter and asks that question, the apparent answer is that God is creator.[31] Thus, some element of that creativity is instilled in man. God created the cosmos. He declared that what He had done was "very good." He then put man within creation. Man responded creatively. He was able to see things with aesthetic judgment (2:9). His cultivation of the garden involved creativity, not monotonous servitude (2:15). He creatively assigned names to the animals (2:19-20). And he was able to respond with poetic expression upon seeing Eve, his help-mate (2:23). Kenneth Myers writes: "Man was fit for the cultural mandate. As the bearer of his Creator-God's image, he could not be satisfied apart from cultural activity. Here is the origin of human culture in untainted glory and possibility. It is no wonder that those who see God's redemption as a transformation of human culture speak of it in terms of re-creation."[32]

As we seek to transform culture we must understand this mandate and apply it.

Pluralism

Pluralism and *secularism* are two prominent words that describe contemporary American culture. The Christian must live within a culture that emphasizes these

---

[31] Dorothy L. Sayers, *The Mind of the Maker* (San Francisco: Harper & Row, 1941), 22.

[32] Kenneth A. Myers, *All God's Children and Blue Suede Shoes* (Westchester, Ill.: Crossway, 1989), 38.

terms. What do they mean and how do we respond? We will look at pluralism first.

The first sentence of professor Allan Bloom's provocative and controversial book, *The Closing of the American Mind*, reads: "There is one thing a professor can be absolutely certain of: almost every student entering the university believes, or says he believes, that truth is relative."[33]

This statement is indicative of Bloom's concern for the fact that many college students do not believe in absolutes, but the concern goes beyond students to the broader population. *Relativism*, *openness*, *syncretism*, and *tolerance* are some of the more descriptive words for the ways people are increasingly thinking in contemporary culture. These words are part of what I mean by *pluralism*. Many ideas are proclaimed, as has always been the case, but the type of pluralism to which I refer asserts that all these ideas are of equal value, and that it is intolerant to think otherwise. Absurdity is the result. This is especially apparent in the realm of religious thought.

In order for evangelicals to be transformers of culture they must understand that their beliefs will be viewed by a significant portion of the culture as intolerant, antiquated, uncompassionate, and destructive of the status quo. As a result, they will often be persecuted through ridicule, prejudice, social ostracism, academic intolerance, media bias, or a number of other attitudes. Just as with Bloom's statement, the evangelical's emphasis on absolutes is enough to draw a negative response. For example, Jesus said, "I am the way, and the truth, and the life; no one comes to the Father, but through Me" (John 14:6). Such an exclusive, absolute claim does not fit current pluralism. Therefore, the pluralist would contend that Jesus must have meant

---

[33] Allan Bloom, *The Closing of the American Mind*, (New York: Simon & Schuster, 1987), 25.

something other than what is implied in such an egocentric statement.

It is unfortunate that Christians often have been absorbed by pluralism. As Harry Blamires puts it, "We have stopped thinking christianly outside the scope of personal morals and personal spirituality."[34] We hold our beliefs privately, which is perfectly legitimate within pluralism. But we have not been the transformers we are to be. We have supported pluralism, because it tolerates a form of Christianity that doesn't make demands on the culture or call it into question.

Christianity is not just personal opinion; it is objective truth. This must be asserted, regardless of the responses to the contrary, in order to transform culture. Christians must affirm this. We must enter our culture boldly with the understanding that what we believe and practice privately is also applicable to all of public life. Lesslie Newbigin writes: "We come here to what is perhaps the most distinctive and crucial feature of the modern worldview, namely the division of human affairs into two realms– the private and the public, a private realm of values where pluralism reigns and a public world of what our culture calls `facts.'"[35]

We must be cautious of incorrect distinctions between the public and private. We must also influence culture with the "facts" of Christianity. This is our responsibility.

Secularism

Secularism permeates virtually every facet of life and thought. What does it mean? We need to understand

---

[34] Harry Blamires, *The Christian Mind* (Ann Arbor, Mich.: Servant, 1963), 37-38.

[35] Newbigin, "West," 359.

that the word *secular* is not the same as *secularism*. All of us, whether Christian or non-Christian, live, work, and play within the secular sphere. There is no threat here for the evangelical. As Blamires says, "Engaging in secular activities . . . does not make anyone a `secularist', an exponent or adherent of `secularism'."[36] Secularism as a philosophy, a worldview, is a different matter. Blamires continues: "While `secular' is a purely neutral term, `secularism' represents a view of life which challenges Christianity head on, for it excludes all considerations drawn from a belief in God or in a future state."[37]

Secularism elevates things that are not to be elevated to such a high status, such as the autonomy of man. Donald Bloesch states that: "a culture closed to the transcendent will find the locus of the sacred in its own creations."[38] This should be a sobering thought for the evangelical.

We must understand that secularism is influential and can be found throughout the culture. In addition, we must realize that the secularist's belief in independence makes Christianity appear useless and the Christian seem woefully ignorant. As far as the secularist is concerned, Christianity is no longer vital. As Emil Brunner says, "The roots of culture that lie in the transcendent sphere are cut off; culture and civilisation must have their law and meaning in themselves."[39] As liberating as this may sound to a secularist, it stimulates grave concern in the mind of an alert evangelical whose view of culture is founded upon God's precepts. There is a clear dividing line.

How is this reflected in our culture? Wolfhart Pannenberg presents what he believes are three aspects of

---

[36] Blamires, *Christian Mind*, 58.

[37] Ibid.

[38] Bloesch, *Freedom*, 228.

[39] Brunner, *Christianity*, 2.

the long-term effects of secularism. "First of these is the loss of legitimation in the institutional ordering of society."[40] That is, without a belief in the divine origin of the world there is no foundation for order. Political rule becomes "merely the exercising of power, and citizens would then inevitably feel that they were delivered over to the whim of those who had power."[41]

"The collapse of the universal validity of traditional morality and consciousness of law is the second aspect of the long-term effects of secularization."[42] Much of this can be attributed to the influence of Immanuel Kant, the eighteenth-century German philosopher, who taught that moral norms were binding even without religion.[43]

Third, "the individual in his or her struggle towards orientation and identity is hardest hit by the loss of a meaningful focus of commitment."[44] This leads to a sense of "homelessness and alienation" and "neurotic deviations." The loss of the "sacred and ultimate" has left its mark. As Pannenberg writes: "The increasingly evident long-term effects of the loss of a meaningful focus of commitment have led to a state of fragile equilibrium in the system of secular society."[45]

Since evangelicals are a part of that society, we should realize this "fragile equilibrium" is not just a problem reserved for the unbelieving secularist; it is also our problem.

---

[40] Wolfhart Pannenberg, *Christianity in a Secularized World* (New York: Crossroad, 1989), 33.

[41] Ibid.

[42] Ibid., 35.

[43] Ibid.

[44] Ibid., 37.

[45] Ibid., 38.

Whether the challenge is secularism, pluralism, or a myriad of other issues, the Christian is called to practice discernment while actively transforming culture.

CHAPTER 3 Culture and the Bible

Jerry Solomon

This is not a Christian culture. We are living in an environment that challenges us to continually evaluate what it means to live the Christian life. So how do we respond? The answer begins with the Bible. Our view of culture must include biblical insights. In this chapter we will investigate selected passages of Scripture pertaining to culture.

The Golden Calf and the Tabernacle: Judging Culture

Chapters 31-39 of Exodus provide a unique perspective of culture and God's involvement with it. On one hand the work of man was blessed through the artistry of Bezalel, Oholiab, and other skilled artisans as they cooperated to build the tabernacle (35-39). On the other hand, the work of man in the form of the golden calf was rejected by God (31-34). This contrast serves to suggest a guideline with which we can begin to judge culture.

Chapter 31:1-11 contains God's initial instructions to Moses concerning the building of the tabernacle in the wilderness. Two important artisans, Bezalel and Oholiab, are recognized by God as being especially gifted for this work. These men were skilled,[46] creative people who were able to contribute significantly to the

---

[46] The word "skill," which is frequently employed to describe artisans in these chapters (NASB), is from the Hebrew word *hakam*, meaning "wise." One of its main synonyms is *bin*, basically meaning "discernment". Thus, the skillful person is one who, in the minds of the Israelites, was also "wise" and "discerning" in his artistry.

religious/cultural life of the nation of Israel. But at this point in the narrative the scene changes dramatically.

While Moses was on the mountain with God, the people became impatient and decided to make a god, an idol. This prompted an enraged response from both God and Moses. The end result was tragic: three thousand were slain as a result of their idolatry.

Then the attention of the people was directed toward the building of the tabernacle. Chapters 35-39 contain detailed accounts from God pertaining to the tabernacle, and the subsequent work of the skilled artisans, including Bezalel and Oholiab. The finished product was blessed (39:42-43).

In this brief survey of a portion of Israel's history we have seen two responses to the work of man's hands: one negative, the other positive. The people fashioned a piece of art, an idol; the response was negative on the part of God and Moses. The people fashioned another piece of art, the tabernacle; the response was positive and worthy of the blessing of both God and Moses. Why the difference in judgment? The answer is deceptively simple: the intent of the art was evaluated. And it was not a matter of one being "secular" and the other "sacred." Art, the cultural product, was not the problem. "Just as art can be used in the name of the true God, as shown in the gifts of Bezalel, so it can be used in an idolatrous way, supplanting the place of God and thereby distorting its own nature."[47]

Art is certainly a vital element of culture. As a result, we should take the lessons of Exodus 31-39 to heart. Our evaluation of culture should include an awareness of intent without being overly sensitive to form. If not, we begin to assign evil incorrectly. As Carl F.H. Henry says,

---

[47] Gene Edward Veith, *The Gift of Art: The Place of the Arts in Scripture* (Downers Grove, IL: InterVarsity, 1983), 31.

"The world is evil only as a fallen world. It is not evil intrinsically."[48]

These insights have focused on certain observers of cultural objects as seen in art: God, Moses, and the people of Israel. In the first case God and Moses saw the golden calf from one perspective, the people of Israel from another. In the second case all were in agreement as they observed the tabernacle. The people's perception changed; they agreed with God's intent and aesthetic judgement. The lesson is that our cultural life is subject to God.

Entering the Fray

How do you react when you're out of your comfort zone: your surroundings, friends, and family? Do you cringe and disengage yourself? Or do you boldly make the best of the new locality?

The first chapter of Daniel tells of four young men who were transported to a culture other than their own by a conquering nation, Babylonia. Their response to this condition provides us with insights concerning how we should relate to the culture that surrounds us. Daniel, of course, proves to be the central figure among the four. He is the focus of our attention.

Note the following facets of this chapter:

1. Daniel and his friends were chosen by the king of Babylon, Nebuchadnezzar, to serve in his court. They were chosen because of their "intelligence in every branch of wisdom ... understanding ... discerning knowledge ... and ability for serving in the king's court" (v. 4).

---

[48] Carl F.H. Henry, *Christian Personal Ethics* (Grand Rapids: Baker, 1957), 420.

2. They were taught "the literature and language of the Chaldeans" (v. 4).

3. Daniel "made up his mind" that he would not partake of the Babylonian food and drink (v. 8).

4. "God granted Daniel favor and compassion" with his superiors even though he and his friends would not partake of the food (v. 9-16).

5. "God gave them knowledge and intelligence in every branch of literature and wisdom" (v. 17).

6. The king found Daniel and his friends to be "ten times better than all the magicians and conjurers who were in all his realm" (v. 20).

This synopsis provides us with several important observations. First, evidently there was no attempt on the part of Daniel and his friends to totally separate themselves from the culture, in particular the educational system of that culture. This was a typical response among the ancient Jews. These young men were capable of interacting with an ungodly culture without being contaminated by it.

Evangelicals are often paranoid as they live within what is deemed an unchristian culture. Perhaps a lesson can be learned from Daniel concerning a proper response. Of course, such a response should be based on wisdom and discernment. That leads us to our second observation.

Second, even though Daniel and his companions learned from the culture, they did so by practicing discernment. They obviously compared what they learned of Babylonian thought with what they already understood from God's point of view. The Law of God was something with which they were well acquainted. Edward Young's comments on v. 17 clarify this: "The knowledge and intelligence which God gave to them ...

was of a discerning kind, that they might know and possess the ability to accept what was true and to reject what was false in their instruction."[49]

Such perception is greatly needed among evangelicals. A separatist, isolationist mentality creates moral and spiritual vacuums throughout our culture. We should replace those vacuums with ideas that are spawned in the minds of Godly thinkers and doers.

Third, God approved of their condition within the culture and even gave them what was needed to influence it (v. 17).

Evangelicals may be directed by God to enter a foreign culture that may not share their worldview. Or, they may be directed to enter the culture that surrounds them, which, as with contemporary western culture, can be devoid of the overt influence of a Christian worldview. If so, they should do so with an understanding that the Lord will protect and provide. And He will demonstrate His power through them as the surrounding culture responds.

The World in the New Testament

In and *of*: two simple words that can stimulate a lot of thought when it comes to what the Bible says about culture, or the world. After all, we are to be in the world but not of it. Let's see what the New Testament has to say.

The terms *kosmos* and *aion*, both of which are generally translated "world," are employed numerous times in the New Testament. A survey of *kosmos* will

---

[49] Edward J. Young, *The Prophecy of Daniel* (Grand Rapids, MI: Eerdmans, 1949), 48-49.

provide important insights. George Eldon Ladd presents usages of the word:[50]

First, the world can refer to "both the entire created order (Jn. 17:5, 24) and the earth in particular (Jn. 11:9; 16:21; 21:25)."[51] This means "there is no trace of the idea that there is anything evil about the world."[52] Second, "kosmos can designate not only the world but also those who inhabit the world: mankind (12:19; 18:20; 7:4; 14:22)."[53] Third, "the most interesting use of kosmos ... is found in the sayings where the world – mankind – is the object of God's love and salvation."[54]

But men, in addition to being the objects of God's love, are seen "as sinful, rebellious, and alienated from God, as fallen humanity. The kosmos is characterized by wickedness (7:7), and does not know God (17:25) nor his emissary, Christ (1:10)."[55] "Again and again ... the world is presented as something hostile to God."[56] But Ladd reminds us that "what makes the kosmos evil is not something intrinsic to it, but the fact that it has turned away from its creator and has become enslaved to evil powers."[57]

So what is the Christian's responsibility in this evil, rebellious world? "The disciples' reaction is not to be one of withdrawal from the world, but of living in the world,

---

[50] George Eldon Ladd, *A Theology of the New Testament* (Grand Rapids: Eerdmans, 1974). In particular, see chapters 17 and 29.

[51] Ibid., 225.

[52] Ibid.

[53] Ibid.

[54] Ibid., 226.

[55] Ibid.

[56] Everett F. Harrison, Geoffrey W. Bromiley, and Carl F.H. Henry, eds. *Baker's Dictionary of Theology* (Grand Rapids: Baker, 1960), s.v. "World, Worldliness," by Everett F. Harrison.

[57] Ladd, 226.

motivated by the love of God rather than the love of the world."[58] "So his followers are not to find their security and satisfaction on the human level as does the world, but in devotion to the redemptive purpose of God" (17:17, 19).[59]

The apostle Paul related that "'worldliness' consists of worshipping the creature rather than the creator (Rom. 1:25), of finding one's pride and glory on the human and created level rather than in God. The world is sinful only insofar as it exalts itself above God and refuses to humble itself and acknowledge its creative Lord."[60] The world is seen as it should be seen when we first worship its creator.

This summary of *kosmos* contributes several points that can be applied to our survey:

1. The world is hostile toward God; this includes the rebellion of mankind.

2. This hostility was not part of the original created order; the world was created good.

3. This world is also the object of God's redemptive love and Christ's sacrifice.

4. The world is not to be seen as an end in itself. We are always to view culture in the light of eternity.

5. We are to be about the business of transforming the world. "We are not to follow the world's lead but to cut across it and rise above it to a higher calling and style."[61] Or, as Ronald Allen says: "Ours is a world of lechery and war. It is also a world of the good, the

---

[58] Ibid., 227.

[59] Ibid.

[60] Ibid., 400.

[61] R.C. Sproul, *The Holiness of God* (Wheaton: Tyndale House, 1985), 209.

beautiful, and the lovely. Eschew lechery; embrace the lovely– and live for the praise of God in the only world we have!"[62]

We are in need of a balance that does not reject beauty, but at the same time recognizes the ugly. Our theology should entail both. The world needs to see this.

Corinthians and Culture

"You're a Corinthian!" If you had heard that exclamation in New Testament times you would know that the person who said it was very upset. To call someone a Corinthian was insulting. Even non- Christians recognized that Corinth was one of the most immoral cities in the known world.

Paul's first letter to the Corinthians contains many indications of this. The believers in Corinth were faced with a culture which resembled ours in several ways. It was diverse ethnically, religiously, and philosophically. It was a center of wealth, literature, and the arts. And it was infamous for its blatant sexual immorality. How would Paul advise believers to respond to life in such a city?

That question can be answered by concentrating on several principles that can be discovered in Paul's letter. We will highlight only a few of these by focusing on certain terms.

Liberty is a foundational term for Christians entering the culture, but it can be misunderstood easily. This is because some act as if it implies total freedom. But "The believer's life is one of Christian liberty in grace."[63] Paul wrote, "All things are lawful for me, but not all things are

---

[62] Ronald B. Allen, *The Majesty of Man: The Dignity of Being Human* (Portland, OR: Multnomah, 1984), 191.

[63] Henry, 420.

profitable. All things are lawful for me, but I will not be mastered by anything" (6:12, 10:23). It must be remembered, though, that this liberty is given to glorify God. A liberty that condones sin is another form of slavery. Thus, "Whether ... you eat or drink or whatever you do, do all to the glory of God" (10:31). In addition, we must be aware of how our liberty is observed by non-believers. Again, Paul wrote, "Give no offense either to Jews or to Greeks or to the church of God" (10:32).

Conscience is another term that figures prominently in how we enter the culture. We must be very sensitive to what it means to defile the conscience. There must be a sensitivity to what tempts us. "The believer who cannot visit the world without making it his home has no right to visit at his weak points."[64] As a result, we need to cultivate the discipline that is needed to respond to the ways the Spirit speaks through our conscience.

Yet another term is brother. In particular, we should be aware of becoming a "stumbling block" to the person Paul calls a "weaker brother." This does not mean that we disregard what has been said about liberty. "A Christian need not allow his liberty to be curtailed by somebody else. But he is obliged to take care that that other person does not fall into sin and if he would hurt that ther person's conscience he has not fulfilled that obligation."[65] This requires a special sensitivity to others, which is a hallmark of the Christian life.

On many occasions, the Probe staff has experienced the challenge of applying these principles. For example, some of us speak frequently in a club in an area of Dallas, Texas called "Deep Ellum." The particular club in which we teach includes a bar, concert stage, and other things

---

[64] Ibid., 428.

[65] F.W. Grosheide, *Commentary on the First Epistle to the Corinthians* (Grand Rapids, MI: Eerdmans, 1953), 243.

normally associated with such a place. Some refer to the clientele as "Generation Xers" who are often nonconformists. We can use our liberty to minister in the club, but we must do so with a keen awareness of the principles we have discussed. When we enter that culture, which is so different from what we normally experience, we must do so by applying the wisdom found in God's Word to the Corinthians.

Encountering the World

How do you get a hearing when you have something to say? In particular, how do you share the truth of God in ungodly surroundings?

Paul's encounter with Athenian culture (Acts 17:16-34) is illustrative of the manner in which we can dialogue with contemporary culture. His interaction exhibits an ability to communicate with a diversity of the population, from those in the marketplace to the Epicurean and Stoic philosophers. And he exhibits an understanding of the culture, including its literature and art. Paul was relating a model for how we can relate our faith effectively. That is, we must communicate with language and examples that can be understood by our audience.

Verse 16 says that Paul's "spirit was being provoked within him as he was beholding the city full of idols." We should note that the verb translated "provoked" here is the Greek word from which we derive the term paroxysm. Paul was highly irritated. In addition, we should note that the verb is imperfect passive, implying that his agitation was a logical result of his Christian conscience and that it was continuous. The idolatry which permeated Athenian culture stimulated this dramatic response. Application: the idolatry of contemporary culture should bring no less a response from us. Materialism, Individualism, Relativism, and Secularism are examples of ideologies that have become idols in our culture.

Verses 17 and 18 refer to several societal groups: Jews, God- fearing Gentiles, Epicurean and Stoic philosophers, as well as the general population, namely "those who happened to be present." Evidently Paul was able to converse with any segment of the population. Application: as alert, thinking, sensitive, concerned, discerning Christians we are challenged to confront our culture in all of its variety and pluralism. It is easier to converse with those who are like-minded, but that is not our only responsibility.

In verse 18, some of the philosophers call Paul an "idle babbler" (i.e., one who makes his living by picking up scraps). Application: we should realize that the Christian worldview, in particular the basic tenets of the gospel, will often elicit scorn from a culture that is too often foreign to Christian truth. This should not hinder us from sharing the truth.

The narrative of verses 19-31 indicates that Paul knew enough about Athenian culture to converse with it on the highest intellectual level. He was acutely aware of the "points of understanding" between him and his audience. He was also acutely aware of the "points of disagreement" and did not hesitate to stress them. He had enough knowledge of their literary expressions to quote their spokesmen (i.e., their poets), even though this does not necessarily mean Paul had a thorough knowledge of them. And he called them to repentance. Application: we need to "stretch" ourselves more intellectually so that we can duplicate Paul's experience more frequently. The most influential seats in our culture are too often left to those who are devoid of Christian thought. Such a condition is in urgent need of change.

Paul experienced three reactions in Athens (vv. 32-34).

1. "Some began to sneer" (v. 32). They expressed contempt.

2. Some said, "We shall hear you again concerning this" (v. 32).

3. "Some men joined him and believed" (v. 34). We should not be surprised when God's message is rejected; we should be prepared when people want to hear more; and we can rejoice when the message falls on fertile soil and bears the fruit of a changed life.

Conclusion

We have seen that Scripture is not silent regarding culture. It contains much by way of example and precept, and we have only begun the investigation. There is more to be done. With this expectation in mind, what have we discovered from the Bible at this stage?

1. In some measure God "is responsible for the presence of culture, for he created human beings in such a way that they are culture-producing beings."[66]

2. God holds us responsible for cultural stewardship.

3. We should not fear the surrounding culture; instead, we should strive to contribute to it through God-given creativity, and transform it through dialogue and proclamation.

4. We should practice discernment while living within culture.

5. The products of culture should be judged on the basis of intent, not form. Or, to simply further:

---

[66] Charles H. Kraft, *Christianity in Culture* (Maryknoll, NY: Orbis, 1979), 103.

We advance the theory that God's basic attitude toward culture is that which the apostle Paul articulates in I Corinthians 9:19-22. That is, he views human culture primarily as a vehicle to be used by him and his people for Christian purposes, rather than as an enemy to be combatted or shunned.[67] Let us use the vehicle for the glory of God!

---

[67] Ibid.

CHAPTER 4 Worldviews

Jerry Solomon

A friend of mine recently told me of a conversation he had with a good friend we will call Joe. Joe is a doctor. He is not a Christian. This is how the conversation went: "Joe, you're an excellent doctor. You care deeply about your patients. Why do you care so much for people since you believe we have evolved by chance? What gives us value?" Joe was stunned by the question and couldn't answer it. His "worldview" had taken a blow.

The concept of a worldview has received increasing attention for the past several years. Many books have been written on the subject of worldviews from both Christian and non-Christian perspectives. Frequently speakers will refer to the term. On occasion even reviews of movies and music will include the phrase. All this attention prompts us to ask, "What does the term mean?" and "What difference does it make?" It is our intent to answer these questions. And it is our hope that all of us will give serious attention to our own worldview, as well as the worldviews of those around us.

What is a Worldview?

What is a *worldview*? Numerous authors offer a variety of definitions. For example, James Sire asserts that: "A worldview is a set of presuppositions (or assumptions) which we hold (consciously or subconsciously) about the basic makeup of our world."[68]

---

[68] James W. Sire, *The Universe Next Door* (Downers Grove, Ill.: InterVarsity, 1988), 17.

Phillips and Brown state that "A worldview is, first of all, *an explanation and interpretation of the world* and second, *an application of this view to life.* In simpler terms, our worldview is a view *of the world* and a view *for the world.*"[69] Walsh and Middleton provide what we think is the most succinct and understandable explanation: "A world view provides a model *of the world* which guides its adherents *in the world.*"[70] With the realization that many subtleties can be added, this will be our working definition.

The Need for a Worldview

Worldviews act somewhat like eye glasses or contact lenses. That is, a worldview should provide the correct "prescription" for making sense of the world just as wearing the correct prescription for your eyes brings things into focus. And, in either example, an incorrect prescription can be dangerous, even life-threatening.

People who are struggling with worldview questions are often despairing and even suicidal. Thus it's important for us to give attention to the formulation of the proper worldview. Arthur Holmes states that the need for a worldview is fourfold: "the need to unify thought and life; the need to define the good life and find hope and meaning in life; the need to guide thought; the need to guide action."[71] Yet another prominent need for the proper worldview is to help us deal with an increasingly diverse culture. We are faced with a smorgasbord of worldviews, all of which make claims concerning truth.

[69] W. Gary Phillips and William E. Brown, *Making Sense of Your World* (Chicago: Moody Press, 1991), 29.

[70] Brian J. Walsh and J. Richard Middleton, *The Transforming Vision* (Downers Grove, Ill.: InterVarsity, 1984), 32.

[71] Arthur F. Holmes, *Contours of a Worldview* (Grand Rapids: Eerdmans, 1983), 5.

We are challenged to sort through this mixture of worldviews with wisdom. These needs are experienced by all people, either consciously or unconsciously. All of us have a worldview with which we strive to meet such needs. The proper worldview helps us by orienting us to the intellectual and philosophical terrain about us.

Worldviews are so much a part of our lives that we see and hear them daily, whether we recognize them or not. For example, movies, television, music, magazines, newspapers, government, education, science, art, and all other aspects of culture are affected by worldviews. If we ignore their importance, we do so to our detriment.

Testing Worldviews

A worldview should pass certain tests. First, it should be rational. It should not ask us to believe contradictory things. Second, it should be supported by evidence. It should be consistent with what we observe. Third, it should give a satisfying comprehensive explanation of reality. It should be able to explain why things are the way they are. Fourth, it should provide a satisfactory basis for living. It should not leave us feeling compelled to borrow elements of another worldview in order to live in this world.

Components Found in All Worldviews

In addition to putting worldviews to these tests, we should also see that worldviews have common components. These components are self-evident. It is important to keep these in mind as you establish your own worldview, and as you share with others. There are four of them.

1. *Something exists*. This may sound obvious, but it really is an important foundational element of worldview building since some will try to deny it. But a denial is self-

defeating because all people experience cause and effect. The universe is rational; it is predictable.

2. *All people have absolutes.* Again, many will try to deny this, but to deny it is to assert it. All of us seek an infinite reference point. For some it is God; for others it is the state, or love, or power, and for some this reference point is themselves or man.

3. *Two contradictory statements cannot both be right.* This is a primary law of logic that is continually denied. Ideally speaking, only one worldview can correctly mirror reality. This cannot be overemphasized in light of the prominent belief that tolerance is the ultimate virtue. To say that someone is wrong is labeled intolerant or narrow-minded. A good illustration of this is when we hear people declare that all religions are the same. It would mean that Hindus, for example, agree with Christians concerning God, Jesus, salvation, heaven, hell, and a host of other doctrines. This is nonsense.

4. *All people exercise faith.* All of us presuppose certain things to be true without absolute proof. These are inferences or assumptions upon which a belief is based. This becomes important, for example, when we interact with those who allege that only the scientist is completely neutral. Some common assumptions are: a personal God exists; man evolved from inorganic material; man is essentially good; reality is material.

As we talk with people who have opposing worldviews, an understanding of these common components can help us listen more patiently, and they can guide us to make our case more wisely.

Six Worldview Questions

Have you ever been frustrated with finding ways to stir the thinking of a non-Christian friend? We are confident the following questions will be of help. And we are also confident they will stir your thinking about the subject of worldviews.

We will answer these questions with various non-Christian responses. Christian responses will be discussed later in this article.

1. *Why is there something rather than nothing?* Some may actually say something came from nothing. Others may state that something is here because of impersonal spirit or energy. And many believe matter is eternal.

2. *How do you explain human nature?* Frequently people will say we are born as blank slates, neither good nor evil. Another popular response is that we are born good, but society causes us to behave otherwise.

3. *What happens to a person at death?* Many will say that a person's death is just the disorganization of matter. Increasingly people in our culture are saying that death brings reincarnation or realization of oneness.

4. *How do you determine what is right and wrong?* Often we hear it said that ethics are relative or situational. Others assert that we have no free choice since we are entirely determined. Some simply derive "oughts" from what "is." And of course history has shown us the tragic results of a "might makes right" answer.

5. *How do you know that you know?* Some say that the mind is the center of our source of knowledge. Things are only known deductively. Others claim that knowledge is only found in the senses. We know only what is perceived.

6. *What is the meaning of history?* One answer is that history is determined as part of a mechanistic universe. Another answer is that history is a linear stream of events linked by cause and effect but without purpose.

Yet another answer is that history is meaningless because life is absurd.[72]

The alert Christian will quickly recognize that the preceding answers are contrary to his beliefs. There are definite, sometimes startling differences. Worldviews are in collision. Thus we should know at least something about the worldviews that are central to the conflict. And we should certainly be able to articulate a Christian worldview.

Examples of Worldviews

In his excellent book, *The Universe Next Door*, James Sire catalogs the most influential worldviews of the past and present. These are Christian Theism, Deism, Naturalism, Nihilism, Existentialism, Eastern Pantheism, and New Age or New Consciousness.[73]

Deism, a prominent worldview during the eighteenth century, has almost entirely left the scene. The Deist believes in God, but that God created and then abandoned the universe.

Nihilism, a more recent worldview, is alive among many young people and some intellectuals. Nihilists see no value to reality; life is absurd.

Existentialism is prominent and can be seen frequently, even among unwitting Christians. The Existentialist, like the Nihilist, sees life as absurd, but sees human beings as totally free to *make himself* in the face of this absurdity.

Christian Theism, Naturalism, and New Age Pantheism are the most influential worldviews presently in the United States. Now we will survey each of them.

---

[72] Sire, 18.

[73] Ibid.

Christian Theism

Let's return to the six questions we asked earlier and briefly see how the Christian Theist might answer them.

Question: Why is there something rather than nothing?

Answer: There is an infinite-personal God who has created the universe out of nothing.

Question: How do you explain human nature?

Answer: Man was originally created good in God's image, but chose to sin and thus infected all of humanity with what is called a "sin nature." So man's Creator has endowed him with value, but his negative behavior is in league with his nature.

Question: What happens to a person at death?

Answer: Death is either the gate to life with God or to eternal separation from Him. The destination is dependent upon the response we give to God's provision for our sinfulness.

Question: How do you determine what is right and wrong?

Answer: God reveals in the Bible the guidelines for our conduct.

Question: How do you know that you know?

Answer: Reason and experience can be legitimate teachers, but a transcendent source is necessary. We know some things only because God tells us through the Bible.

Question: What is the meaning of history?

Answer: History is a linear and meaningful sequence of events leading to the fulfillment of God's purposes for man.

Christian Theism had a long history in Western culture. This does not mean that all individuals who have lived in Western culture have been Christians. It simply means that this worldview was dominant; it was the most influential. And this was true even among non-Christians. This is no longer valid. Western culture has experienced a transition to what is called Naturalism.

Naturalism

Even though Naturalism in various forms is ancient, we will use the term to refer to a worldview that has had considerable influence in a relatively short time within Western culture. The seeds were planted in the seventeenth century and began to flower in the eighteenth. Most of us have been exposed to Naturalism through Marxism and what is called Secular Humanism.

What are the basic tenets of this worldview? First, God is irrelevant. This tenet helps us better understand the term Naturalism; it is in direct contrast to Christian Theism, which is based on *supernaturalism*. Second, progress and evolutionary change are inevitable. Third, human beings are autonomous, self-centered, and will save himself. Fourth, education is the guide to life; intelligence and freedom guarantee full human potential. Fifth, science is the ultimate provider both for knowledge and morals. These tenets have permeated our lives. They are apparent, for example, in the media, government, and education. We should be alert constantly to their influence.

After World War II, "Postmodernism" began to replace the confidence of Naturalism. With it came the conclusion that truth, in any real sense, doesn't exist. This may be the next major worldview, or anti-worldview, that will infect the culture. It is presently the rage on many of our college campuses. In the meantime, though, the past few decades have brought us another ancient worldview dressed in Western clothing.

New Age Pantheism

Various forms of Pantheism have been prominent in Eastern cultures for thousands of years. But it began to have an effect on our culture in the 1950s. There had been various attempts to introduce its teachings before then, but those attempts did not arouse the interest that was stirred in that decade. It is now most readily observed in what is called the New Age Movement.

What are the basic tenets of this worldview? First, all is one. There are no ultimate distinctions between humans, animals, or the rest of creation. Second, since all is one, all is god. All of life has a spark of divinity. Third, if all is one and all is god, then each of us is god. Fourth, humans must discover their own divinity by experiencing a change in consciousness. We suffer from a collective form of metaphysical amnesia. Fifth, humans travel through indefinite cycles of birth, death, and reincarnation in order to work off what is called "bad karma." Sixth, New Age disciples think in terms of gray, not black and white. Thus they believe that two conflicting statements can both be true.

On the popular level these tenets are presently asserted through various media, such as books, magazines, television, and movies. Perhaps the most visible teacher is Shirley MacLaine. But these beliefs are also found increasingly among intellectuals in fields such as medicine, psychology, sociology, and education.

Conclusion

We have very briefly scanned the subject of worldviews. Let's return to a definition we affirmed in the beginning of this article: "A worldview provides a model *of the world* which guides its adherents *in the world*." If your model of the world includes an infinite-personal God, as in Christian Theism, that belief should provide guidance for your life. If your model rejects God, as in Naturalism, again such a belief serves as a guide. Or if your model asserts that you are god, as in New Age Pantheism, yet again your life is being guided by such a conception. These examples should remind us that we are living in a culture that puts us in touch constantly with such ideas, and many more. They cannot all be true.

Thus, some of us may be confronted with the need to think more deeply than we ever have before. Some of us may need to purge those things from our lives that are contrary to the worldview of Christian Theism. Some of us may need to better understand that our thoughts are to be unified with daily life. Some of us may need to better understand that the good life and hope and meaning are found only through God's answers. Some of us may need to let God's ideas guide our thoughts more completely. And some of us may need to let God's guidelines guide our actions more fully.

Paul's admonition to the believers in ancient Colossae couldn't be more contemporary or helpful in light of our discussion. He wrote:

> See to it that no one takes you captive through philosophy and empty deception, according to the tradition of men, according to the elementary principles of the world, rather than according to Christ (Col. 2:8).

CHAPTER 5 Worldviews Through History

Kerby Anderson

How have worldviews changed throughout history? This chapter provides a perspective against which to compare and contrast a Christian, biblical worldview based on New Testament principles.

Roman Worldview

In order to explain how the worldviews we talk about developed through history, we will be using the book written by Professor Glenn Sunshine, *Why You Think the Way You Do: The Story of Western Worldviews from Rome to Home.*[74]

Glenn Sunshine is a member of the church that Jonathan Edwards attended when he was at Yale. Professor Sunshine gave a lecture about Jonathan Edward's worldview at a conference they held, and Chuck Colson invited him to teach with the Centurions program. He gave a talk about "How We Got Here" and then later turned it into *Why You Think the Way You Do*.

Since we will be talking about worldview, it would be good to begin with Glenn Sunshine's definition. "A worldview is the framework you use to interpret the world and your place in it."[75] You do not need to be a philosopher to have a worldview. All of us have a worldview.

---

[74] Glenn Sunshine, *Why You Think the Way You Do: The Story of Western Worldviews from Rome to Home* (Grand Rapids, MI: Zondervan, 2009).

[75] Ibid., 13.

Although Glenn Sunshine begins with the worldview of the Roman world, he quickly takes us back to Neo-Platonism. It was the religion and philosophy based upon Plato's ideas. Neo-Platonism was the belief that the fundamental ground of reality is non-physical. Instead it is found in the world of ideas (and is known as *idealism*). These ideas cast shadows that cast other shadows until they arrive at the physical world.

According to this worldview, the whole universe exists as a hierarchy. The spiritual is superior to the physical. This provides a scale of values for the world, but also provides a scale for humanity. In other words, those who are superior should rule over those who are inferior because they have demonstrated their ability to rule or conquer.

This view of hierarchy led to the idea of the father having superiority over all members of the family. It led to the idea that men are superior to women. It led to the idea that the emperor should rule and be worshipped. And it led to the idea that slaves are inferior to free people and nothing more than "living tools."[76]

This explains not only the success of Rome but also its ugly underside. Essentially, there are two pictures of Rome: "the glittering empire and the rotten core."[77]

In Rome, human life did not have much value. While it is true that Romans abandoned human sacrifice, they engaged in other practices equally abhorrent. "They picked up the Etruscan practice of having people fight to the death in games in honor of the dead."[78]

Slavery provided the economic foundation for the empire. Abortion and infanticide were regularly

---

[76] Ibid., 31.

[77] Ibid., 20.

[78] Ibid., 30

practiced. "Roman families would usually keep as many healthy sons as they had and only one daughter; the rest were simply discarded."[79] And Roman law required that a father kill any visibly deformed child.

Transformation of the Pagan World

How did Christianity transform the pagan world? In AD 303, the Roman emperor Diocletian began a severe persecution of Christians. But because Christians were faithful and even willing to go to their deaths for their beliefs, their credibility increased. Eventually they were accepted and allowed to exercise their faith. Constantine even legalized the Christian faith by AD 313.

Once that took place, Christian ideas were allowed to percolate through society. One of the most important ideas was that human beings are created in the image of God. This idea has a profound impact. First, it meant that people are fundamentally equal to each other. No longer were there grounds for saying that some people are superior to others. In fact, "Christians were the first people in history to oppose slavery systematically."[80]

Christians (who believed that all are created in the image of God) treated the sick differently. They believed that even those who were deathly ill still deserved care. Dionysius of Alexandria reported that Christians (often at great risk to their own lives) "visited the sick fearlessly and ministered to them continually."[81] They would rescue babies abandoned in an act of infanticide. They would oppose abortion.

In economics, we can also see the influence of Christianity. The idea that God created the universe and

[79] Ibid., 33-34.

[80] Ibid., 43.

[81] Ibid., 44.

then rested showed that God worked. That would mean that human beings (made in the image of God) are expected to work as well. God gave Adam and Eve intellectual work (in naming the animals) and physical work (in tending the Garden). Contrast this with the Roman world where physical work was seen as something that only slaves would do. Christians saw labor as something that was intrinsically valuable.

Labor is good; drudgery is bad. Drudgery is a result of the Fall (Genesis 3). So Christians were the first to develop technology to remove drudgery from work. Other civilizations had technology, but the West uniquely applied such things as waterpower to make work more valuable and worthwhile by eliminating the drudgery and repetitive nature of certain tasks.

Property rights were also well developed during this period. "The medieval world under the influence of Christianity has a much stronger emphasis on property rights than other cultures had."[82]

These ideas come from a biblical worldview and began to be developed during the Middle Ages. This led to a complete transformation of western society and set it on a trajectory to our modern world.

Christianity and Politics

Glenn Sunshine points out that in the West, the dynamic between church and state is unique. Christianity was originally a persecuted minority religion. Even when Christianity was declared a legal religion, the church did not depend upon the state. So the question of the relationship between church and state has been an open question.

---

[82] Ibid., 76.

During the Middle Ages, two men helped shape political thinking. The first was Augustine, who described two realms: the City of God and the City of Man. He argued that human government is the result of sin. He believed that it is based upon selfishness. Government itself is corruption. In the absence of government, anarchy reigns. So government is a necessary evil.

The City of God is different in that it is not based upon force or coercion. It is based upon love, charity, and repentance. That doesn't mean that the City of Man and the City of God cannot work together. But overall, Augustine had a more pessimistic view of government.

Aristotle had a different view of government. As people in the Middle Ages began to rediscover Aristotle, they began to develop a different view of government. They saw government as a necessary institution that God has placed in the world. It had positive and legitimate functions.

Aristotle believed that government had a more positive role in society. But the Christian theologians had to also deal with the problem of original sin. They wanted to find a way to prevent original sin from corrupting the government. The tension between these two views is what drives the discussion of western political theory.

Sunshine notes, "another check on civil government involved the idea of rights."[83] We normally associate the idea of rights, especially inalienable rights, with eighteenth century political theorists. However, John Locke's idea that we have inalienable right to life, liberty, and property is already found in the writings of medieval theologians. The basis for this is a belief that all are created in the image of God. Therefore, all of us have a number of natural rights that the state cannot remove.

---

[83] Ibid., 91.

Natural law was the idea that God wove moral laws into the fabric of the universe.

There also was the belief that there should be limitations on the jurisdiction of civil government and church government. One example is the Magna Carta, that stated that the English church was to be free and its liberties unimpaired by the crown.

Renaissance and Enlightenment

What about the transformation into the modern world? In the early modern period, starting with the Renaissance in the fifteenth century to the seventeenth century, there are a whole series of events that shook the worldview consensus that developed in the Middle Ages.

Previously there were certain beliefs about truth: (1) that truth was absolute, (2) that truth is knowable to the human mind, and (3) that truth is necessary for society (a society could not be based upon a lie). The best good guide for truth would be the great civilizations of the past that lasted for so long and thus must have been based upon truth.

The idea was to go to the past to find truth. During the Renaissance scholars were very successful in collecting manuscripts and finding ancient sources. Unfortunately, they found so many sources that they discovered there was not a coherent perspective. The ancient writers disagreed with each other. In a sense, the Renaissance was a victim of its own success. There was too much information. The more ancient sources they found, the less likely they would find agreement in the perspectives. Once it became obvious that this grand synthesis was not possible, the entire purpose of intellectual activity was thrown into question.

Then there were the wars of the Reformation in which various factions fought over who was the true follower of the prince of peace. The devastation of the religious wars left many people wondering if there really was religious certainty. No longer was the question "is Christianity true" but rather "which Christianity is true?" Now you had a multiplicity of options that left people confused. This also generated questions about the role of religion in society.

Then you also had the discovery of the New World and whole people groups that had never heard the gospel. Some began to ask questions like: Is it fair of God to send them all to hell because they had never heard of Christianity? Or, in light of biblical history, where did they come from? How do these people fit with the story of Noah? These discoveries called into question biblical morality and biblical history.

Also, people started using a new way of looking at knowledge. They began to use the scientific method to evaluate everything. This begins a significant shift in how we understand the world. There is a movement away from certainty toward probability. There is also a movement away from studying ancient authors toward scientific experimentation.

In the modern world, therefore, truth is not found in the past but in the present and future. With this is also questioning of biblical authority.

The Modern World and Christianity

Let me conclude by talking about our modern world and how Christians should respond. Sunshine concludes his book with chapters on "Modernity and Its Discontents" and "The Decay of Modernity." Essentially the modern world has left humans with a loss of truth, certainty, and meaning in life. "Materialism provides a ready answer to the question of the meaning and purpose of life: there is none."[84] From a Darwinian perspective, our only purpose is to pass our genes on to the next generation.

This rejection of spirituality and meaning has ushered in various other worldviews as alternatives. These would be such worldviews as postmodernism, neo-paganism, and the New Age Movement. Sunshine argues that in many ways we have been catapulted back to Rome.

Like Rome, we value toleration as the supreme virtue. Rome believed that toleration was important because it kept the empire together. If you go beyond the lines of toleration, you are persecuted. This is similar to the mindset today. The highest value in a postmodern world is toleration. Toleration so defined means that we will embrace any and all lifestyles people may choose.

The Romans lived in an oversexed society.[85] So do we. Rome practiced abortion. So does our society. Rome was anti-natal and made a deliberate attempt to prevent pregnancy. They focused on sexual enjoyment and did not want to bother with kids. In our modern world, birthrates in most of the western democracies are plummeting.

Western civilization is a product of ancient Roman civilization plus Christianity. Sunshine argues that once you removed Christianity, modern society reverted back to Roman society and a recovery of the ancient pagan worldview.

So how should Christians live in this world? Of course, we should live out a biblical worldview. Every

---

[84] Ibid., 177.

[85] Ibid., 33.

generation is called to live faithfully to the gospel, and our generation is no exception.

This is especially important today since we are facing a society that is not willing to accept biblical ideas. In many ways, we face a challenge similar to the early church, though not as daunting. From history, we can see that the early church did live faithfully and transformed the Roman world. Christians produced a totally new civilization: western culture. By living faithfully before the watching world, we will increase our credibility and earn the respect from those who are around us by living in accordance with biblical principles.

SECTION 2 ART

What is art? How should a Christian evaluate the arts? What does the Bible say about art and music? Can a Christian be involved in producing art, music, or film?

CHAPTER 6 Art and the Christian

Jerry Solomon and Jimmy Williams

Art in our Lives

Where are you as you read this? You may be sitting in an office, reclining in a lounge chair at home, lounging in your back yard, sitting at a desk in your dorm room, or any other of a number of scenarios. Consider for a moment if art is part of your consciousness. If you are sitting in an office, is art anywhere within your vision? If you are reclining in a lounge chair, does the furniture have an artistic dimension? If you are lounging in your back yard, can the word art be used to describe any facet of what you see? If you are in your dorm room, are you listening to music that is art?

If I had the pleasure of talking with you about these questions, no doubt we would have a very interesting conversation. Some of you may say, "No, art doesn't describe anything I see at the moment." Or, some of you may state, "I haven't thought of this before. You'll have to give me more time for reflection." Others may assert, "I only think of art within museums, concert halls or other such places that enshrine our art." Others may say, "Yes, art is very much a part of my daily life." But since I can't dialog with you in order to know what you are doing at the moment, and I certainly cannot see what you see, let me tell you where I am and what I see as I write these comments.

I am sitting in my study at my desk while I am listening to the music of Bach. I see a clock on one of the bookshelves, a hand-painted plate I purchased in the

60

country of Slovenia, a framed poem given to me by my daughter, several chairs, two floor lamps, a mirror with a bamboo frame, two canoe paddles I bought in the San Blas islands off the coast of Panama, a wooden statue I purchased in Ecuador, and a unique, colorful sculpture that was made by my son. As I mention these things, perhaps you are attempting to imagine them. You are trying to "see" or "hear" them and in so doing there are certain of these items you may describe as art.

Your first response may be to say that the music of Bach, the hand-painted Slovenian plate, or the Ecuadorian statue can be described as art. But what about the chair in which I am sitting, the desk, the bookshelves, the chairs, or the lamps? Better yet, what about such items that are found where you live? Are they art?

Such questions are indicative of the challenges we face when we begin to consider the place of art in our lives. As an evangelical Christian I can state that art and the aesthetic dimensions of life have not received much attention within my formal training. Only through my own pursuit have I begun to think about art with a Christian worldview. And I have found my experience is similar to what many have experienced within the evangelical community. Too often we have tended to label art as inconsequential or even detrimental to the Christian life.

Actually, there is nothing new about this. Our spiritual forefathers debated such issues. They were surrounded by Greek and pagan cultures that challenged them to give serious thought to how they should express their new beliefs. Art surrounded them, but could the truth of Christ be expressed legitimately through art? Could Christians give positive attention to the art of non-Christians? In light of such struggles it is my intention to encourage you to give attention to some of the basic elements of a Christian worldview of art and aesthetics in this essay. I believe you will find that our discussion can have significant application in your life.

Art and Aesthetics

Several years ago I was having dinner with a group of young people when our conversation turned to the subject of music. During the discussion I made a comment about how I believe there is a *qualitative* difference between the music of Bach and that of a musician who was popular among Christians at the time of our discussion. When one of the group at our table heard this, he immediately responded in anger and accused me of flagrant prejudice and a judgmental spirit. Even though I attempted to elaborate my point, the young man had determined that I was an elitist and would not listen any longer.

This incident serves as a reminder that one of the most prevalent ways of approaching art is to simply say that "beauty is in the eye (or ear) of the beholder." The incident also serves to show that concepts of "good" and "bad," or "beautiful" and "ugly," or other adjectives, are part of our vocabulary when we talk of art. This is true whether we believe such terms apply only to individuals or everyone. The vocabulary pertains to a field of philosophy called aesthetics.

All of us deal with aesthetics at various times in our lives, and many of us incorporate aesthetic statements in daily conversations. For example, we may say, "That was a *great* movie." Or, "That was a *terrible* movie." When we make such statements we normally don't think seriously about how such terms actually apply to what we have seen. We are stating our opinions, but those opinions are usually the result of an immediate emotional response. The challenge comes when we attempt to relate *qualitative* statements about the movie as part of a quest to find universal guidelines that can be applied to all art. When we accept this challenge we begin to explain why some artists and their art is great, some merely good, and others not worthwhile.

Aesthetics and Nature

Perhaps one of the clearest ways to begin to understand the aesthetic dimension of our lives is to consider how we respond to nature. Have you ever heard anyone say, "That's an *ugly* sunset." Probably not, but surely you have heard the word *beautiful* applied to sunsets. And when you hear the phrase "beautiful sunset" you probably don't hear an argument to the contrary. Usually there is a consensus among those who see the sunset: it is beautiful. From a Christian perspective those who are there are offering a judgment concerning both the "artist" and the "art." Both the "cause" and "effect" have been praised aesthetically. Torrential waterfalls, majestic mountains, as well as sunsets routinely evoke human aesthetic response. The Christian knows that the very fabric of the universe expresses God's presence with majestic beauty and grandeur. Psalm 19:1 states, "The heavens declare the glory of God and the firmament shows forth his handiwork." Nature has been called the "aesthetics of the infinite." Through telescope or microscope, one can devote a lifetime to the study of some part of the universe—the skin, the eye, the sea, the flora and fauna, the stars, the climate. All of nature can be appreciated for its aesthetic qualities which find their source in God, their Creator. In fact, we can assert that "the major premise of a Christian worldview, including a Christian aesthetic, is that God is the Creator."[86]

---

[86] C. Nolan Huizenga, "The Arts: A Bridge Between the Natural and Spiritual Realms," in *The Christian Imagination*, ed. Leland Ryken (Grand Rapids, Mich.: Baker, 1981), 70.

Human Creativity

"You have a wonderful imagination! Are you an artist?" Has anyone said such things to you? If so, perhaps you responded by saying something that would reject the person's perception of you. Most of us don't see ourselves as imaginative, artistic people. Indeed, most of us tend to think of the artist and imagination as terms that apply only to certain elite individuals who have left a legacy of work. "The truth is that in discussing the arts we are discussing something universal to mankind."[87] For example, anthropologists tell us all primitive peoples thought art was important.[88] Why is this true?

From the perspective of a Christian worldview the answer is found in how we are created. Since we are made in God's image that must include the glorious concept that we too are creative. After creating man, God told him to subdue the earth and rule over it. Adam was to cultivate and keep the garden (Gen. 2:15) which was described by God as "very good" (Gen. 1:31). The implication of this is very important. God, the Creator, a lover of the beauty in His created world, invited Adam, one of His creatures, to share in the process of "creation" with Him. He has permitted humans to take the elements of His cosmos and create new arrangements with them. Perhaps this explains the reason why creating anything is so fulfilling to us. We can express a drive within us which allows us to do something all humans uniquely share with their Creator.

God has thus placed before the human race a banquet table rich with aesthetic delicacies. He has supplied the basic ingredients, inviting those made in His image to exercise their creative capacities to the fullest

---

[87] Nicholas Wolterstorff, *Art in Action* (Grand Rapids, Mich.: Eerdmans, 1980), 4.

[88] Ibid.

extent possible. We are privileged as no other creature to make and enjoy art.

There is a dark side to this, however, because sin entered and affected all of human life. A bent and twisted nature has emerged, tainting every field of human endeavor or expression and consistently marring the results. The unfortunate truth is that divinely-endowed creativity will always be accompanied in earthly life by the reality and presence of sin expressed through a fallen race. Man is Jekyll and Hyde: noble image-bearer and morally-crippled animal. His works of art are therefore bittersweet.

Understanding this dichotomy allows Christians to genuinely appreciate something of the contribution of every artist, composer, or author. God is sovereign and dispenses artistic talents upon whom He will. While Scripture keeps us from emulating certain lifestyles of artists or condoning some of their ideological perspectives, we can nevertheless admire and appreciate their talent, which ultimately finds its source in God.

The fact is that if God can speak through a burning bush or Balaam's donkey, He can speak through a hedonistic artist! The question can never be how worthy is the vessel, but rather has truth been expressed? God's truth is still sounding forth today from the Bible, from nature, and even from fallen humanity.

Because of the Fall, absolute beauty in the world is gone. But participation in the aesthetic dimension reminds us of the beauty that once was, and anticipates its future luster. With such beauty present today that can take one's breath away, even in this unredeemed world, one can but speculate about what lies ahead for those who love Him!

Art and the Bible

What does the Bible have to say about the arts? Happily, the Bible does not call upon Christians to look down upon the arts. In fact, the arts are *imperative* when considered from the biblical mandate that whatever we do should be done to the glory of God (I Cor. 10:31). We are to offer Him the best that we have— intellectually, artistically, and spiritually. Further, at the very center of Christianity stands the *Incarnation* ("the Word made flesh"), an event which identified God with the physical world and gave dignity to it. A real Man died on a real cross and was laid in a real, rock-hard tomb. The Greek ideas of "other- worldly-ness" that fostered a tainted and debased view of nature (and hence aesthetics) find no place in biblical Christianity. The dichotomy between sacred and secular is thus an alien one to biblical faith. Paul's statement, "Unto the pure, all things are pure" (Titus 1:15) includes the arts. While we may recognize that human creativity, like all other gifts bestowed upon us by God, may be misused, there is nothing inherently or more sinful about the arts than other areas of human activity.

The Old Testament

The Old Testament is rich with examples which confirm the artistic dimension. Exodus 25 shows that God commanded beautiful architecture, along with other forms of art (metalwork, clothing design, tapestry, etc.) in the building of the tabernacle and eventually the temple. Here we find something unique in history art works conceived and designed by the infinite God, then transmitted to and executed by His human apprentices!

Poetry is another evidence of God's love for beauty. A large portion of the Old Testament, including Psalms, Proverbs, Ecclesiastes, Song of Solomon, portions of the prophets, and Job contain poetry. Since God inspired the very words of Scripture, it logically follows that He inspired the poetical form in such passages.

Music and dance are often found in the Bible. In Exodus 15 the children of Israel celebrated God's Red Sea victory over the Egyptians with singing, dancing, and the playing of instruments. In 1 Chronicles 23:5 we find musicians in the temple, their instruments specifically made by King David for praising God. And we should remember that the lyrical poetry of the Psalms was first intended to be sung.

The New Testament

The New Testament also includes artistic insights. The most obvious is the example of Jesus Himself. First of all, He was by trade a carpenter, a skilled craftsman (Mark 6:3). Secondly, His teachings are full of examples which reveal His sensitivity to the beauty all around: the fox, the bird nest, the lily, the sparrow and dove, the glowering skies, a vine, a mustard seed. Jesus was also a master story-teller. He readily made use of His own cultural setting to impart His message, and sometimes quite dramatically. Many of the parables were fictional stories, but they were nevertheless used to teach spiritual truths via the imagination.

We should also remember that the entire Bible is not only revelation, it is itself a work of art. And this work of art "has been the single greatest influence on art. It sheds more light upon the creative process and the use of the arts than any other source, because in it are found the great truths about man as well as God that are the wellsprings of art."[89]

---

[89] Frank E. Gaebelein, "Toward a Biblical View of Aesthetics," in The Christian Imagination, ed. Leland Ryken (Grand Rapids, Mich.: Baker, 1981), 48-49.

Evaluating Art

Can the Bible help us evaluate art? Consider the concepts found in Philippians 4:8:

Finally, brethren, whatever is true, whatever is honorable, whatever is right, whatever is pure, whatever is lovely, whatever is of good repute, if there is any excellence and if anything worthy of praise, let your mind dwell on these things.

Let's concentrate for a few moments on this verse in order to see if it might at least provide the beginning of a framework for the evaluation and enjoyment of art.

Paul begins with *truth*. When considering art the Christian is compelled to ask, "Is this really true?" Does life genuinely operate in this fashion in light of God's revelation? And Christians must remember that truth includes the negatives as well as the positives of reality.

The second word refers to the concept of *honor* or *dignity*. This can refer to what we related earlier in this essay about the nature of man: we have dignity even though we are sinful. This gives a basis, for example, to reject the statements in the work of the artist Francis Bacon. Bacon painted half-truths. He presented deterioration and hopeless despair, but he didn't present man's honor and dignity.

The third key to aesthetic comprehension has to do with the moral dimension—what is *right*. Not all art makes a moral statement, but when it does Christians must deal with it, not ignore it. For example, Picasso's painting, Guernica, is a powerful moral statement protesting the bombing by the Germans of a town by that name just prior to World War II. Protesting injustice is a cry for justice.

Purity is the fourth concept. It also touches on the moral– by contrasting that which is innocent, chaste, and pure from that which is sordid, impure, and worldly. For instance, one need not be a professional drama critic to identify and appreciate the fresh, innocent love of Romeo and Juliet, nor to distinguish it from the erotic escapades of a Tom Jones.

While the first four concepts have dealt with facets of artistic statements, the fifth focuses on sheer beauty: "Whatever is *lovely*." If there is little to evaluate morally and rationally, we are still free to appreciate what is beautiful in art.

The sixth concept, that of *good repute*, gives us impetus to evaluate the life and character of the artist. The less than exemplary lifestyle of an artist may somewhat tarnish his artistic contribution, but it doesn't necessarily obliterate it. The greatest art is true, skillfully expressed, imaginative, and unencumbered by the personal and emotional problems of its originators.

Excellence is yet another concept. It is a comparative term; it assumes that something else is not excellent. The focus is on quality, which is worth much discussion. But one sure sign of it is craftsmanship: technical mastery. Another sign is durability. Great art lasts.

The last concept is *praise*. Here we are concerned with the impact or the effect of the art. Great art can have power and is therefore a forceful tool of communication. Herein lies the "two-edged swordness" of art. It can encourage a culture to lofty heights, and it can help bring a culture to ruin. Paul undergirds this meaty verse by stating that we should let our minds "dwell on these things," a reminder that Christianity thrives on intelligence, not ignorance even in the artistic realm.

Thus, it is my hope that we will pursue the artistic dimensions of our lives with intelligence and imagination. The world needs to see and hear from Christians committed to art for the glory of God.

CHAPTER 7 Music and the Christian

Jerry Solomon

Music is a pervasive part of contemporary culture. We hear it on elevators, in restaurants, on telephones while we wait for our party to answer, in offices, in hotel lobbies, and in virtually every corner of contemporary life. In fact, it permeates the airwaves so thoroughly we often do not realize it is there. Television uses music not only in musical programs but also in commercials and program soundtracks. Movies also utilize music to enhance the events shown on the screen. Radio offers a wide variety of music around the clock. The availability of recordings allows us to program music to suit our own listening tastes, and we can hear them in virtually any location. Concerts, especially in large cities, offer a potpourri of music to choose from.

There are also a wide variety of musical genres. Rock (with its assortment of styles and labels), rap, country and western, jazz, Broadway, folk, classical, New Age, and gospel provide us with a dizzying assortment of listening and performing options. Such permeation and variety provide us with a unique opportunity to practice discernment. Some may think this is unnecessary because they claim to listen only to "Christian" music. Nevertheless, the broader population of the evangelical community spends innumerable hours absorbing music, whether "Christian" or "secular."

Why should a Christian be interested and involved in the arts, music in particular? In his excellent work *Theology and Contemporary Art Forms*, John Newport lists several helpful points:

The first reason Christians should be interested in the arts is related to the biblical teaching that God reveals and carries on his redemptive purpose in time and history. The Christian community ...cannot cut itself off from the characteristic artistic vitalities of history–past and present. Second...the arts give a peculiarly direct access to the distinctive tone, concerns, and feelings of a culture.... The artists not only mirror their age in its subtlest nuances, but they generally do it a generation ahead of more abstract and theoretical thinkers. Third...the arts focus (in a remarkably vivid and startling way) on the vital issues and themes which are the central concern of theology. Fourth...the arts spell out dramatically the implications of various worldviews.[90]

The second, third, and fourth points are especially applicable to music. If music mirrors culture, if it tells us of important issues and themes; and if it shows the implications of various worldviews, it can tell us a great deal about our culture. Lyrically, music can be used as a medium for criticism, commendation, reflection, questioning, rebellion, and any number of other thoughts or emotions. When the musical language is employed to relay these thoughts or emotions the result can be significant.

History is replete with examples of the ways music has been vitally employed in various cultures. One of the more prominent examples of this can be found in the Psalms, where lyrics were merged with music to form a strategic voice for Israel's life. The same is true in contemporary life. The themes of rock, rap, and country

---

[90] John P. Newport, *Theology and Contemporary Art Forms* (Waco, Tex.: Word, 1971), 17-24.

music demonstrate how music can be a notable voice for the spirit of a culture, whether for good or evil.

In order to affect our culture we must listen to that voice. We must hear its questions and be sensitive to the needs that cry out for the answers God provides.

Can Music Be "Christian"?

One of the continuing debates among Evangelicals centers on how music is to be judged. Some say there is a particular musical style that is distinctly Christian. Others reject such a proposition. Some believe that certain musical styles are intrinsically evil. Others reject this. The examples of such conflict are numerous. It is important that we join the dialogue. In the process we will observe several ways we should respond to the music of our culture.

First, the term "Christian music" is a misnomer. Music cannot be declared Christian because of particular ingredients. There is no special Christian musical vocabulary. There is no distinctive sound that makes a piece of music Christian. The only part of a composition that can make it Christian is the lyrics. In view of the fact that such phrases as "contemporary Christian music" are in vogue, this is a meaningful observation. Perhaps the phrase "contemporary Christian lyrics" would be more appropriate. Of course, the lyrics may be suspect doctrinally and ethically, and they may be of poor quality, but my point is concentrated on the musical content.

It is possible that misunderstandings regarding "Christian music" are the product of cultural bias. Our "western ears" are accustomed to certain sounds. Particular modes, scales, and rhythms are part of a rich musical heritage. When we hear music that is not part of that heritage, we are tempted to label it, inaccurately, as unfit for a Christian's musical life.

We should realize that music is best understood within its culture. For example, the classical music of India includes quartertones, which are foreign to our ears. They generally sound very strange to us, and they are often played on instruments that have a strange sound, such as the sitar. But we would be guilty of flagrant prejudice if we were to maintain that such music is un- Christian because it does not contain the tones we are used to hearing. Another example of the way evangelicals tend to misapply the term Christian to music can be understood by reflecting on how music may have sounded during biblical and church history. Scholars have begun to demonstrate that the music of biblical history may have been comprised of tonal and rhythmic qualities that were very different from what we are accustomed to in western culture.

The attitudes of Luther and Calvin toward the use of music show a disagreement concerning the truth of a particular Christian style. Charles Garside provides intriguing insights:

> Luther had openly proclaimed his desire to use all available music, including the most obviously secular, for the worship of the church. . . . Calvin, to the contrary, now absolutely rejects such a deployment of existing musical resources.[91]

It is obvious that these great men did not agree on the nature of music.

Our musical preconceptions do not die easily, and they seem to recur periodically in church history. Once a

---

[91] Charles Garside, Jr., *The Origins of Calvin's Theology of Music: 1536-1543* (Philadelphia: American Philosophical Society, 1979), 19.

style becomes familiar enough, it is accepted. Until then, it is suspect. More recent examples can be found in the controversies surrounding the use of instruments such as drums and guitars during worship services. Evangelicals need to be alert to their biases and understand that "Christian music" is a misnomer.

The "Power" of Music

It is often claimed that music has "power" to manipulate and control us. If this were true, Skinnerian determinism would be correct in asserting that there is no such thing as personal choice or responsibility. Music, along with other "powers" found in our cultural settings, would be given credit that is not legitimate.

Best and Huttar address this by saying:

> The fact that music, among other created and cultural things, is purported by primitives and sophisticates alike to have power is more a matter of the dislocation of priorities than anything else.[92]

Such beliefs not only stimulate a "dislocation of priorities," they also stimulate poor theology.

The Bible tells us that early in their relationship David played music for King Saul. On one occasion what Saul heard soothed him, and on another occasion the same sounds infuriated him. In reality, though, the reactions were Saul's decisions. He was not passive; he was not being manipulated on either occasion by the "power" of the music.

Much contemporary thinking places the blame for aberrant behavior (sexual misconduct, rebellion, violence,

---

[92] Zondervan Pictorial Dictionary, s.v. "Music," by Harold M. Best and David Huttar.

etc.) on the supposed intrinsic potency of music to orchestrate our actions. Some extend this to the point of believing that music is the special tool of Satan, so when such behavior is exhibited he is the culprit. Again, Best and Huttar offer pertinent thoughts. They write:

> Ultimately the Judeo-Christian perspective maintains that man is interiorly wrong and that until he is right he will place the blame for his condition outside himself.[93]

Admittedly, my point is a subtle one. We must be careful not to imply music cannot be used for evil purposes. But we must realize that the devil goads people who use music; he does not empower the music itself.

Current controversy among Christians concerning the rhythmic content of rock music is an example of the tendency to believe that some musical styles are intrinsically evil. For example, Steve Lawhead has demonstrated that the music of the early slaves probably did not include much rhythmic substance at all. The plantation owners would not have allowed drums because they could have been used to relay messages of revolt between the groups of slaves. This observation is central to the issue of rock music, because some assert that the syncopated rhythm of rock is the product of the pagan African backgrounds of the slaves. In reality, American slave music centered around the playing of a "banya," an instrument akin to the banjo, and not drums or other rhythmic instruments.[94]

Rock music is not intrinsically evil. It did not originate in a pagan past, and even if it did that would not mean that it is evil. Nevertheless, since it has been a prominent and influential part of American culture for

---

[93] Ibid.

[94] Steve Lawhead, *Rock of This Age* (Downers Grove, Ill.: InterVarsity, 1987), 51-52.

several decades, it demands the attention of evangelicals. The attention it is given should begin with the understanding that the problems that are a part of rock do not reside in the music itself; they reside in sinful people who can and often do abuse it. The same can be said about any musical style, or any other art form.

The Quality of Music

So far, I have asserted two propositions concerning how Christians can respond to the music of their culture: the term Christian music is a misnomer, and no musical style is intrinsically evil. While both of these statements are true, they say nothing about the quality of music we choose to make a part of our lives. Thus my third proposition is that music should be evaluated based on quality. A proposal that includes judgments of quality is a challenging one. Evangelicals will find this especially difficult, because the subject of aesthetics is not a prevalent part of our heritage.

Evangelicals tend toward lazy thinking when it comes to analyzing the music of their culture. As Frank Gaebelein said, "It is more difficult to be thoughtfully discriminating than to fall back upon sweeping generalization."[95] There are several factors to be weighed if discriminating thought is to occur.

We should focus attention on the music within Christian life. This applies not only to music used in worship, but also to music heard via radio, CDs, concerts, and other sources.

Lack of quality is one of the themes of those who write about contemporary church music. Harold Best

---

[95] Frank E. Gaebelein, "The Christian and Music," in *The Christian Imagination: Essays on Literature and the Arts*, ed. Leland Ryken (Grand Rapids, Mich.: Baker, 1981), 446.

states: "Contentment with mediocrity as a would-be carrier of truth looms as a major hindrance to true creative vision among evangelicals."[96]

Robert Elmore continues in a similar vein:

> There are even ministers who feed their congregations with the strong meat of the Word and at the same time surround their preaching with only the skimmed milk of music.[97]

If negative declarations such as these are the consensus of those who have devoted ardent attention to the subject, what are the contents of a positive model? The answers to this are numerous. I will only relate some of the insights of one thinker, Calvin Johansson.

The first insight refers to movement. Music must move. The principle here is that music needs to exhibit a flow, an overall feel for continuity, that moves progressively and irresistibly from beginning to end. It is not intended to hammer and drive a musical pulse into the mind. This principle can be applied to the incessant nature of the rock rhythm.

The second insight has to do with cohesion. Unity is an organic pull, a felt quality that permeates a composition so thoroughly that every part, no matter how small, is related.

The third insight relates to "diversions at various levels.... Without diversity there would only be sameness, a quality that would be not only boring but also devastatingly static."

---

[96] Harold M. Best, "Christian Responsibility in Music," in *The Christian Imagination*, 402.

[97] Robert Elmore, "The Place of Music in Christian Life," in *The Christian Imagination*, 430.

The fourth insight focuses on "the principle of dominance.... A certain hierarchy of values is adopted by the composer in which more important features are set against the less important." The fifth insight shows that "every component part of a composition needs to have intrinsic worth in and of itself.... The music demonstrates truth as each part of the composition has self-worth."[98]

These principles contain ideas that the non-musician might find difficult to understand. Indeed, most of us are not accustomed to using language to discuss the quality of the music we hear other than to say we do or do not "like" it. But if we are going to assess the music of the broader culture accurately, we must be able to use such language to assess music within our own subculture. We must seek quality there.

Pop Music

Another factor in musical discrimination applies to the way we approach music outside our subculture. The Christian is free to enter culture equipped with discernment, and this certainly applies to music. We need not fear the music of our culture, but we must exercise caution.

Assessments of quality also apply here. The Christian should use the principles we discussed above to evaluate the music of the broader culture.

We should also be aware of the blending of music and message, or lack of it. The ideal situation occurs when both the medium and the message agree.

Too often, the music we hear conveys a message at the expense of musical quality. Best explains:

---

98 Calvin M. Johansson, *Music and Ministry: A Biblical Counterpoint* (Peabody, Mass.: Hendrickson, 1984), 93-95.

The kind of mass communication on which the media subsist depends on two things: a minimal creative element and a perspective that sees music only as conveying a message rather than being a message. Viewed as a carrier, music tends to be reduced to a format equated with entertainment. The greater the exposure desired, the lower the common denominator.[99]

The messages of our culture are perhaps voiced most strongly and clearly through music that is subordinated to those messages. The music is "canned." It is the product of cliches and "hooks" designed to bring instant response from the listener. As Erik Routley stated, "All music which self-consciously adopts a style is like a person who puts on airs. It is affected and overbearing."[100] This condition is so prevalent in contemporary music it cannot be overemphasized.

Another concern is found in certain features of what is usually called "popular culture." Music is a major part of pop culture. Kenneth Myers, among others, has identified certain culture types beginning with "high," diminishing to "folk," and plummeting to "popular." Popular culture "has some serious liabilities that it has inherited from its origins in distinctively modern, secularized movements."

Generally, these liabilities include "the quest for novelty, and the desire for instant gratification."[101] In turn, these same qualities are found in "pop" music.

---

[99] Ibid., 412-13.

[100] Erik Routley, *Church Music and the Christian Faith*, (Carol Stream, Ill.: Agape, 1978), 89.

[101] Kenneth Myers, *All God's Children and Blue Suede Shoes: Christians and Popular Culture* (Westchester, Ill.: Crossway, 1989), 59-64.

The quest for novelty is apparent when we understand, as Steve Lawhead states, that the whole system feeds on the "new"—new faces, new gimmicks, new sounds. Yesterday in pop music is not only dead; it is ancient history.[102]

The desire for instant gratification is the result of the fact that this type of music is normally produced for commercial reasons. Continuing, Lawhead writes that

> ... commercialism, the effective selling of products, governs every aspect of the popular music industry. From a purely business point of view, it makes perfect sense to shift the focus from artistic integrity to some other less rigorous and more easily managed, non artistic component, such as newness or novelty. Talent and technical virtuosity take time to develop, and any industry dependent upon a never-ending stream of fresh faces cannot wait for talent to emerge.[103]

We do not offer God our best when we employ this approach. Additionally, we do not honor God when we make the products of such thinking a consistent part of our lives.

[102] Steve Lawhead, *Turn Back the Night: A Christian Response to Popular Culture* (Westchester, Ill.: Crossway, 1978), 97.

[103] Ibid., 98.

CHAPTER 8 Film and the Christian

Todd Kappelman

The Convergence of High and Low Culture

An examination of the history of our century will reveal the importance of viewing and studying film for any individuals who wish to understand themselves and their time and place. Film is essential because the distinction so many make between so called "high" and "low" culture has in fact disappeared (if it ever existed in the first place).

Approximately one hundred years ago the dawn of electronic technology, beginning with the invention of the radio, gave birth to mass media and communications. The increase in leisure time and wealth fostered the birth and development of an entertainment industry. The decline in the quality of education and the explosion in the popularity of television sealed the union between what was traditionally considered "high" art and popular culture. Western society is now defined more strictly by the image, the sound, and the moving picture than by the written word, which defined previous centuries. Seldom does anyone ask, "What have you read lately?" One is much more likely to hear the question, "What have you seen lately."

We have become, for better or worse, a visually oriented society. Because literature is no longer the dominant form of expression, scriptwriters, directors, and actors do more to shape the culture which we live in than do the giants of literature or philosophy. We may

82

be at the point in the development of Western culture that the Great Books series needs to be supplemented by a Great Films series.

The church as a body has a long standing and somewhat understandable tradition of suspicion concerning narrative fiction, the concepts of which apply here to our discussion of film. A brief examination of positions held by some Christians from the past regarding written fictional narratives may help us to understand the concern some have with involvement in fictional narratives as recorded on film.

Alcuin, an influential Christian leader of the ninth century was extremely concerned about the worldliness he saw in the church. One of the things that troubled him the most was the monks' fondness for fictional literature and stories about heroes such as Beowulf and Ingeld. Writing to Higbald, Alcuin said: "Let the words of God be read aloud at the table in your refractory. The reader should be heard there, not the flute player; the Fathers of the Church, not the songs of the heathen . . . . What has Ingeld to do with Christ?"[104]

Tertullian, the father of Latin theology, writing six centuries earlier voiced a similar concern about Christians involved in secular matters when he said: "What has Athens to do with Jerusalem?"[105] Specifically, Tertullian believed that the study of pagan philosophers was detrimental to the Christian faith and should be avoided at all costs.

Paul, the apostle, writing to the Church at Corinth (2 Corinthians 6:14-15) asked: "What partnership does righteousness have with iniquity? Or what fellowship has light with darkness? What accord has Christ with Belial?"

---

[104] "Letter to Higbald," as quoted in Eleanor S. Duckett, *Alcuin, Friend of Charlemagne* (New York:Macmillan, 1951), 209.

[105] Tertullian, *On the Against Heretics*, chap. 7.

83

Conclusion: The objections raised against the arts, both past and present, do have merit and should not be dismissed too quickly. Christians have a right and a responsibility to make sure that entertainment and art are not used in a manner that is damaging to their spiritual welfare. It is often a difficult call. For example, many Christians objected to the work of Federico Fellini and Ingmar Bergman in the fifties and sixties, yet men such as Francis Schaeffer thought that it was necessary to pay attention to what these individuals were saying and why.

The Nature of Film and the Opportunity for Christians

Properly understood film is a narrative medium, a kind of "visual book" with a beginning, middle, and ending that contains some degree of resolution. All film is not created equal; some movies are made with the express purpose of providing diversionary entertainment, while others represent the sincere efforts of artists to make works of art that reflect human emotions and call people to a more reflective existence. This second category of film should be considered an art form and is therefore worthy of the same attention that any other art such as the ballet, sculpture, or painting receives.

Art is the embodiment of man's response to reality and his attempt to order his experience of that reality.[106] Man has always and will continue to express his hope and excitement, as well as his fears and reservations about life, death, and what it means to be human through the arts. He will seek to express his world through all available means, and presently that includes film. Schindler's List, a recent film by Steven Spielberg, is

---

[106] John Dixon, Jr., *Nature and Grace in Art*, as quoted in Leland Ryken's *The Liberated Imagination*, p.23.

an excellent example of film's ability to express man's hopes and fears.

As a picture of reality, film is able to convey an enormous range of human experiences and emotions. The people one encounters in films are frequently like us whether they are Christian or not. Often the people we see in the better films are struggling with some of the most important questions in life. They are attempting to find meaning in what often appears to be a meaningless universe. These people are often a vehicle used by a director, producer, or writer to prompt us to ask the larger questions of ourselves.

Film is not and should not be required to be "uplifting" or "inspiring." Christians should remember that non-Christians also have struggles and wrestle with the meaning of life and their place and purpose in the universe. Christians and non-Christians will not and should not be expected to come to the same conclusions to the problems they face in the fictional universe of film. The Scriptures indicate that Christians and non-Christians are different, and this should be a point of celebration, not alarm, for the Christian audience.

T. S. Eliot, speaking about literature, but with much that can be applied to film, had this advice for the Christian:

> Literary criticism should be completed from a definite ethical and theological standpoint.... It is necessary for Christian readers [and film goers by extension], to scrutinize their reading, [again film by extension], especially of works of imagination, with explicit ethical and theological standards.[107]

---

[107] T. S. Eliot, *Religion and Literature*.

Therefore, Christians should take their worldview with them when they attend and comment on any film. They should be cautious about pronouncing a film that does not conform with Christian beliefs or their particular notion of orthodoxy as unfit for consumption or undeserving of a right to exist as art.

Conclusion: The need for participation in film arises from not only the diversity of material with which the medium deals, but also from the plurality of possible interpretations concerning a given film. Christians have an opportunity to influence their culture by entering the arena of dialogue provided by film and contending for their positions and voicing their objections with sophistication, generosity, and a willingness to hear from those of opposing beliefs.

Some Concerns about Christian Participation in Cinema[108]

Christians are often concerned about the content of certain films and the appropriateness of viewing particular pieces. This is a valid concern that should not be dismissed too quickly and certainly deserves a response from those who do view objectionable material. The two primary areas of concern leveled by the many detractors of contemporary culture as it pertains to film are found in the categories of gratuitous sex and violence. It is crucial that Christians understand the exact nature of sex and violence, gratuitous and otherwise, and how it may be employed in art. Taking only violence as the representative issue of these two concerns, we must ask ourselves what, if any, redeeming value does it have, and can it be used and viewed under some circumstances?

---

[108] Much of the material for this section was first articulated by Jeff Hanson, my co-editor, in the March/April issue of The Antithesis, vol. 1, no. 2, 1995.

We might turn to the use of gratuitous violence in literature in order to better understand the role of violence in film. If the former is understood and embraced (albeit with reservation), the latter may also be understood and embraced (again with caution) as a means of expression employed by a new image-driven culture.

The image of gratuitous violence in modernity has one of its first and most important articulations in *The Rime of the Ancient Mariner*, by Samuel Taylor Coleridge. Recall that in the poem the sailor shoots an albatross for absolutely no reason and is condemned by his fellow sailors, who believed the bird was a good omen, to wear the dead body around his neck. The ship is ravaged by plague, and only the cursed mariner survives. After many days of soul searching on the ghost ship, the mariner pronounces a blessing upon all of creation and atones for his wrongs. A sister ship saves the man, and he begins to evangelistically tell his story to anyone who will listen.

Every time this poem is read in a class or other group there is invariably some person who is fixated on the act of violence and emphasizes it to the point of losing the meaning of the entire poem. The story is about a mariner who realizes the errors of his ways, repents, and comes to a restored relationship with creation and other men. For Coleridge, the act of violence thus becomes the vehicle for the turning of the character's soul from an infernal orientation to the paradisal. Other authors have used similar methods. Dante, for example, repeats a similar pattern when he explored the spiritual realms in his poetic chronicle *The Divine Comedy*. First, he takes his readers through the harshness, pain, and misery of the Inferno before moving into Purgatory and finally into the bliss and joy of Paradise. Dostoyevsky composed four novels that begin with the heinous crime of Raskolnikov and develop to the salvation of the Karamazov brothers.

Conclusion: The writers mentioned here and many serious, contemporary film makers often explore the darkness of the human condition. They don't do it simply to posture or exploit, but to see deeply and lay bare the problems and tensions. But, they also do it to look for answers, even the light of salvation/Salvation. The picture is not always pretty, and the very ugliness of the scene is often necessary to accurately portray the degree of depravity and the miracle of salvific turns in fiction. By virtue of their full acquaintance with the dark side of the human condition, when they propose solutions, these solutions appear to be viable and realistic.

Biblical Examples of Gratuitous Violence

The prohibition against and objections to the use of violence in film may be understood better through an examination of the use of violence in the Bible.

One example found in Scriptures is in the thirteenth chapter of the book of Isaiah. In verses fifteen and sixteen the prophet is forecasting the particulars of the future Assyrian military invasion and the conditions the people of Israel and the surrounding countries will experience. He writes:

> Whoever is captured will be thrust through; all who are caught will fall by the sword. Their infants will be dashed to pieces before their eyes; their houses will be looted and their wives ravished (Isaiah 13:15-16).

The prophet is talking about the impaling of men by the conquering armies, the willful smashing of infants upon the rocks, and the raping of women. In an oral and textual based society, those who heard the words of Isaiah would have been able to imagine the horrors he described and would have made mental images of the scenes.

In an image-driven society if this scene were to be part of a movie, a scriptwriter and director would have actors and actresses play the parts, and the violence would be obvious to all. Recall the scene in The Ten Commandments where the Egyptian armies attempted to follow Moses across the Red Sea. One sees horses and soldiers trapped under tons of water. Their bodies go limp before they can get to the surface. And those who can make it to the top face certain death trying to swim back to shore. In spite of these, and other horrific scenes, this movie is often held to be a "Christian classic" and deemed to be a good family film by many.

A second and even more disturbing example of gratuitous violence in the Bible is found in the twentieth chapter of Judges. Here a Levite and his concubine enter the house of an old man from the hill country of Ephraim to spend the night. While they are there, some wicked men in the city want to have homosexual relations with the Levite traveler and demand that the old man hand them over. The evil men take the man's concubine, rape and kill her, leaving her dead body in the doorway. The traveler is so distraught that he cuts his concubine into twelve pieces and sends the body parts back to his fellow Israelites. The Israelites then form a revenge party and go into battle with the Benjamites who will not turn over the evil men for punishment.

Again, if this story were to be translated into a visual medium the scenes of rape and later dismemberment of a body, even if they were filmed in standards from the forties or fifties, would be very disturbing.

Conclusion: The purpose of the violence in these examples may be that the details in each passage provide information that serves as a reason for a latter action. Or, the information provided shows us something about the

89

nature of God and the way He deals with sin. If both these examples show a difficult, but necessary use of violence in telling a story, then perhaps violence may be used (portrayed) for redemptive purposes in fictional mediums such as film. This is not an airtight argument, rather the issue is raised as a matter for consideration while keeping in mind that Christians should always avoid living a vicariously sinful life through any artistic medium.

Weaker Brother Considerations in Viewing Film

Paul's great teaching concerning meat sacrificed to idols and the relationship of the stronger and weaker brothers to one another is laid out in 1 Corinthians 8. We should remember that Paul clearly puts the burden of responsibility on the stronger brother. It is this person who should have the interest of the weaker brother in mind.

Persons who exercise rampant Christian freedom when watching films that are objectionable to some others does not necessarily mean that they are strong Christians. It could indicate that these people are too weak to control their passions and are hiding behind the argument that they are a stronger brother. Do not urge others to participate in something that you, as a Christian, feel comfortable doing if they have reservations. You may inadvertently cause the other person to sin.

There are basically three positions related to Christians viewing film.

The first of these three is prohibition. This is the belief that films, and often television and other forms of entertainment, are inherently evil and detrimental to the Christian's spiritual wellbeing. Persons who maintain this position avoid all film, regardless of the rating or reputed benefits, and urge others to do the same.

Abstinence is the second position. This is the belief that it is permissible for Christians to view films, but for personal reasons this person does not choose to do so. This may be for reasons ranging from a concern for the use of time or no real desire to watch film, to avoidance because it may cause them or someone they are concerned about to stumble. Willingly abstaining from some or all films does not automatically make one a weaker brother, and this charge should be avoided! One should avoid labeling a fellow Christian "weaker" for choosing to abstain from participation in some behavior due to matters of conscience.

Moderation is the final position. This is the belief that it is permissible to watch films and that one may do so within a certain framework of moderation. This person willingly views some films but considers others to be inappropriate for Christians. There is a great deal of disagreement here about what a Christian can or cannot and should or should not watch. Although some of these disagreements are matters of principle and not of taste, Christian charity should be practiced whenever one is uncertain.

Conclusion: There is a valid history of concern about Christian involvement in the arts and fictional and imaginative literature. This issue extends to the medium of film and manifests similar concerns about film and Christians who view film. However, because film is one of the dominant mediums of cultural expression, film criticism is necessary. If Christians do not make their voices heard then others, often non-Christians, will dominate the discussion. All films contain the philosophical persuasions of the persons who contribute to their development, and it is the job of the Christian who participates in these arts to make insightful, fair, and well-informed evaluations of the work. Not everyone feels comfortable in viewing some (or any) films and the Christian should be especially mindful of the beliefs of others and always have the interest of fellow believers as well as non-believers in mind. While "film," the artistic expression of the cinematic medium has been the focus and not "movies," the entertainment based expression, much of what has been said of the former is applicable to the later.

Tempering Christian Freedom with Restraint

Christians should be aware that the freedoms exercised in participation in the film arts are privileges and should not be practiced to the point of vicarious living through escape into fictitious worlds. In 1 Corinthians 10: 23-31 (and 6:12) the Apostle Paul writes that: "everything is permissible, but not everything is constructive."

He is addressing the issue of meat sacrificed to idols in chapter 10 and sexual purity in chapter 6. This may serve as a guide for Christians who are concerned about their involvement in film and a caution against construing what is written here as a license to watch anything and everything. The Apostle is very careful to distinguish between that which is permissible and that which is constructive, or expedient. What Paul means is that, in Christ, believers have freedoms which extend to all areas of life, but these freedoms have the potential to be exercised carelessly or without regard for others, and thus become sin. The guiding rule here is that Christians should seek the good of others and not their own desires. This would mean that anyone who is participating in film that is objectionable should have the interests of others, both believers and non-believers, in mind. We live in a fallen world and almost everything we touch we affect with our fallen nature, the arts notwithstanding. If we are to be active in redeeming the culture for the glory of God, then by necessity we must participate in the culture and be salt and light to a very dark and unsavory world.

It is imperative that Christians who are active in their culture and interested in participating in the ever growing "culture wars," remember Paul's admonition in Philippians that we "work out our salvation daily with fear and trembling." Anything less would be flirting with spiritual disaster and would not bring glory to God.

Parents concerned for the spiritual and psychological welfare of their children would do well to offer more than a list of prohibitions against what films can be viewed. As with anything that involves issues of Christian freedom, maturity in individual matters must be taken into account. The example of a young child's first BB gun may serve as an illustration. In some instances a child may be ready for the first air rifle at age twelve or thirteen. Other children may not be ready until they are eighteen, and some may best served if they never possess the gun in question. Parents should realize that film is a narrative medium which often contains complex philosophical ideas. To continue to absorb films at the current rate and not offer thoughtful criticism on what we are watching is equivalent to visiting museums and announcing that the Picasso or Rembrandt retrospective is "cool" or "stupid." If we are concerned parents, and wish to gain the respect of our children, we can and must do better than this.

Section 3 - Media

How can a Christian live a godly life in the midst of the media storm that surrounds us each day? How should we evaluate the entertainment in our lives? What forms of media are affecting our view of the world?

CHAPTER 9 Is It Just Entertainment?

Jerry Solomon

Picture a grocery store in your mind. There are many aisles filled with a variety of products. Fresh fruit, vegetables, canned foods, bread, cereal, meat, dairy products, frozen foods, soap, and numerous other items can be found. When we shop in such a store we need to be aware of certain things. These may include the price, size, weight, variety, brand, quality, and freshness. After analyzing all of this, we are left with the most important part of the shopping trip–the decision! We must decide which of the products we will buy.

Our world is a lot like a grocery store. There are a variety of ideas (worldviews) to be considered. Those ideas can be seen and heard through television, music, movies, magazines, books, billboards, and bumper stickers, and other sources. In a sense, we are shopping in the grocery store of ideas. As Christians, we need to be aware of the products. We need to consider what is being sold. Then we need to decide if we should make a purchase.

Most of us want to be physically healthy. Unfortunately, sometimes we don't eat as if that were true. The same is true of our minds. We want to be mentally healthy. But too often we don't "eat" as if that were true! Our minds are often filled with things that are unhealthy. This can be especially true of the entertainment we choose.

How can we become more aware of the products and make the right purchases when we "go shopping" in the world of entertainment? It is our intent to help answer this question.

A Christian is usually encouraged to think of God's Word, the Bible, as the guide for life. Of course the challenge of such a position is found in practice, not theory. Living by the tenets of Scripture is not always an easy thing. And we can be tempted to think that God's ideas are restrictive, negative, and life-rejecting. The "don'ts" of biblical teachings can appear to overshadow a more positive, life-affirming perspective.

Does God Intend for Us to Enjoy Life?

Think of a series of three questions. First, if you make the Bible your standard for living, do you think that means life will be dull? Some Christians tend to live as if the answer is "yes." This certainly applies to entertainment. It appears that we are to be so separate from the world that we can't enjoy any part of it. Second, if you wrote a song, a poem, a novel, or if you painted a picture, sculpted a statue, etc., do you think you would know best how it should be sung, read, or understood? Of course the answer is "yes." It came from your mind and imagination. You "brought it to life." Third, if God created all things and knows everything about you, do you believe He knows how to bring true joy into your life? Again, the answer is obviously "yes." You came from His mind and imagination. He "brought you to life." He knows best how you should be sung, read, and understood. And He relays that information through His word, the Bible. He wants you to enjoy life, but with His guidelines in mind.

What is God's Will for Entertainment?

Just what are those guidelines? What is God's will for us concerning entertainment?

Before this question is answered, it is important to understand that the Bible clearly teaches God's will for much of life. Too often we tend to think of pursuing God's will for reasons that include such things as a particular occupation or marriage partner, and other such important decisions that are not stated clearly in Scripture. But the Bible frequently teaches the will of God for daily living in obvious ways. The following passages demonstrate this:

- "A wise man is cautious and turns away from evil, but a fool is arrogant and careless" (Prov. 14:16).

- "Let us behavior properly as in the day, not in carousing and drunkenness, not in sexual promiscuity and sensuality, not in strife and jealousy" (Rom. 13:13).

- "Flee immorality" (1 Cor. 6:18a).

- "Finally, brethren, whatever is true, whatever is honorable, whatever is right, whatever is pure, whatever is lovely, whatever is of good repute, if there is any excellence and if anything worthy of praise, let your mind dwell on these things" (Phil. 4:8).

- "See to it that no one takes you captive through philosophy and empty deception, according to the tradition of men, according to the elementary principles of the world rather than according to Christ" (Col 2:8).

- "Put them all aside: anger, wrath, malice, slander, and abusive speech from your mouth" (Col. 3:8).

- "Now flee from youthful lusts, and pursue righteousness, faith, love and peach, with those who call on the Lord from a pure heart" (2 Tim. 2:22).

Obviously various types of contemporary entertainment are not mentioned in these verses. The Bible "does not endeavor to specify rules for the whole of life."[109] Thus we are challenged to make decisions about entertainment based upon the application of biblical principles. The Christian must know the "principles for conduct: which apply here, which do not, and why. Then he must decide and act. Thus, by this terrifying and responsible process, he matures ethically. There is no other way."[110] In fact, this process signifies our continual spiritual growth, or sanctification. As Hebrews 5:14 states: "Solid food is for the mature, who because of practice have their senses trained to discern good and evil." Most of us probably don't think of "training our senses," but such a concept surely should be a part of our thinking continually.

Years ago I had an opportunity to demonstrate the use of "trained senses" when I attended a heavy metal rock concert at the invitation of a sixteen-year-old friend. He was a new Christian then, and we were spending a lot of time together. He had entered his new life after years of attachment to a certain popular rock musician who was the main act of the concert.

During the evening the musicians heavily emphasized the themes of sex, drugs, and violence, and

---

[109] Carl F. H. Henry, *Christian Personal Ethics* (Grand Rapids, Mich.: Baker, 1957), 419.

[110] Ibid.

the crowd of adolescents and pre- adolescents was encouraged to respond, and did. After awhile I asked my friend how Jesus would respond to what we heard and saw. His response indicated that for the first time he had begun to think about this form of entertainment—which had been very important to him—with Christian principles in mind.

Perhaps the most succinct statement of Christian ethical principles is found in 1 Corinthians 10:31: "Whether, then, you eat or drink or whatever you do, do all to the glory of God." Can you think of anything more than "whatever" or "all"? These all-encompassing words are to be applied to all of life, including our entertainment choices. My young friend made this discovery that night.

What Types of Entertainment Are Evil?

The answer to this question is not always simple. Perhaps the best response is one that doesn't put much stress on the medium itself. For example, the rhythm of rock music is not evil; television is not evil; movies are not evil; video games are not evil; novels are not evil, etc.

Of course, it is possible for some to claim, for instance, that pre-marital sex is legitimate entertainment. But the clear admonition of Scripture forbids such activity. And the underlying point is that sex is not intrinsically evil. The one who is engaged in such activity is taking what is good and misusing it for evil. So evil does not reside in sex, rock music, television, etc. Types of entertainment are conduits for good or evil. People are evil. People who provide entertainment and people who use it can abuse it. A basic premise of theology is that man has a sin nature. We are prone to abuse all things. As Genesis 8:21 states, "The intent of man's heart is evil from his youth."

What About Content?

So the Christian is free to make entertainment a part of his life with an understanding that evil resides in people, not forms. But caution and discernment must be applied. We must be alert to the importance of our minds and what they can absorb through entertainment.

Perhaps we need to stop doing some of the things we normally do while listening to music, watching television, etc., so we can concentrate on the ideas that are entering our minds. We might be amazed at the ideas we'll notice if we take the time to concentrate. For example, an old TV commercial says, "Turn it loose! Don't hold back"! We may want to ask what "it" refers to, and we may want to know what is to be "held back." Such a commercial is a thinly veiled espousal of hedonism; an ancient philosophy that says pleasure is the ultimate good. Ideas are powerful, and they have consequences, even when they come from something as seemingly innocuous as a TV commercial.

Consider the following illustration. Think of your mind as a sponge. A sponge absorbs moisture not unlike the way your mind absorbs ideas. (The difference is you are making choices and the sponge is not.) In order to remove the moisture, you must squeeze the sponge. If someone were to do the same with your "sponge brain," what would come out? Would you be embarrassed if the Lord were to be present? Biblical teaching says He is always present. If we honor Him, we'll enjoy life in the process.

If we are using our minds and thinking Christianly about entertainment we will be more alert concerning content. All entertainment is making a statement. A

100

worldview, or philosophy of life, is being espoused through what we read, hear, or watch. Movies, for example, can range from the introspective existential comedies of Woody Allen to the euphoric pantheistic conjectures of Shirley MacLaine. We are challenged to respond to such content with our Christian worldview intact.

Are We in a Battle?

We must take care of our minds. A battle is taking place in the marketplace of ideas. Entertainment can be seen as one of the battlefields where ideas are vying for recognition and influence. As 2 Corinthians 10:5 states, "We are destroying speculations and every lofty thing raised up against the knowledge of God, and we are taking every thought captive to the obedience of Christ." And Colossians 2:8 warns us: "See to it that no one takes you captive through philosophy and empty deception, according to the tradition of men, according to the elementary principles of the world, rather than according to Christ."

What About the Conscience?

We should also consider the place of the conscience. We must be aware of the possibility of defiling our conscience (1 Cor. 8:7). As Paul wrote in 1 Corinthians 6:12, "All things are lawful for me, but not all things are profitable." The believer who cannot visit the world without making it his home has no right to visit it at his weak points.[111] It is the responsibility of each of us to be sensitive to what the conscience is telling us when we encounter those weak points and respond in a way that honors God.

---

[111] Ibid., 428.

Thus, I suggest three steps in cultivating sensitivity to our consciences.

1. Consider what our conscience is relating *prior* to the entertainment. Is there something about what we've heard or seen that brings discomfort? If so, it may be a signal to stay away from it.

2. Consider the conscience *during* the entertainment. If we're already watching and listening, are we mentally and spiritually comfortable? If not, we may need to get away from it. Unfortunately, too often the tendency is to linger too long and in the process we find that what may have disturbed us previously is now taken for granted.

3. Consider the conscience *after* the entertainment. Now that it's over, what are we thinking and feeling? We should be alert to what the Lord is showing us about what we have just made a part of our lives.

What Do Others Say?

In addition to an awareness of the conscience, we may benefit from what others have to say. Perhaps the advertising will provide information that will prove to be of help before we decide to participate. Frequently ads will tell us things about the content and the intent of the producers. Also, we may find it beneficial to be alert to what friends may say. The things we hear from them may indicate warning signs, especially if they are Christian friends who are attempting to apply biblical principles to their lives. In addition, some objective critics can offer insightful comments. There are ministries around the country, for example, dedicated to analyzing the latest movies. And there are others that attempt to cover a broader spectrum of entertainment from a Christian perspective. You may benefit from subscribing to their publications.

Of course, this encouragement to consider what others say cannot exempt us from personal responsibility. To rely completely on others is an unhealthy practice that can lead to mental and spiritual stagnation. Each of us must be mentally and spiritually alert to the content of entertainment.

Isn't It "Just Entertainment"?

Maybe you've heard someone say, "It's just entertainment"! Is this true?

The principles we have affirmed can lead to several common objections. Our answers to these objections can help us gain additional insight into how we think about contemporary entertainment.

1. Some people say that what has been shown in a movie or some other entertainment is "just reality." But is reality a legitimate guideline for living? Do we derive an "ought" from an "is"? Saying that reality has been portrayed says nothing about the way things ought to be from God's perspective. Reality needs analysis and it often needs correction.

2. A common statement is, "I'm just killing time." The person who says this may be doing exactly that, but what else is being killed in the process? The Christian redeems time; he doesn't kill it. As Ephesians 5:15-16 states, "Be careful how you walk, not as unwise men, but as wise, making the most of your time, because the days are evil."

3. "It won't affect me" is a common objection. Tragically, these can be the proverbial "famous last words" for some. Ted Bundy, a serial killer who was executed for his crimes, began to look at pornography when he was very young. If you had warned him of the potential consequences of his actions in those early years,

he probably would have said it wouldn't affect him. We can't predict the outcome of our actions with absolute clarity. In addition, we may not recognize the consequences when they appear because we have been blinded subtly over a period of time.

4. Other people say, "There's nothing else to do." This is a sad commentary on contemporary life. If that is true, then God has done a poor job of supplying us with imagination. Spending hours watching TV each day, for instance, says a great deal about our priorities and use of our God-given abilities and spiritual gifts.

5. Young people in particular tend to say, "Everybody's doing it." It is highly doubtful that is true. More importantly, though, we must understand that God's principles don't rely on democracy. We may be called to stand alone, as difficult as that may be.

6. Some people say, "No one will know." Humanly, this is absurd. The person who says this knows. He's somebody, and he has to live with himself. And if he is a Christian his worldview informs him that God knows. Is he trying to please God or himself?

7. "It's just entertainment" can be the response. No, it's not just entertainment. We can't afford to approach contemporary entertainment with the word just. There is too much at stake if we care about our minds, our witness, and our future.

So what should we do? Should we become separatists? No, the answer to the challenge of entertainment is not to seclude ourselves in "holy huddles" of legalism and cultural isolation. Should we become consumers? No, not without discernment. As we said in the beginning of this series, when it comes to entertainment, we should be as selective in that "grocery store of ideas" as we are in the food market. Should we become salt and light? Yes! We are to analyze entertainment with a Christian worldview, and we are to "infect" the world of entertainment with that same vision.

CHAPTER 10 Sex and Violence on Television

Kerby Anderson

Is there too much sex and violence on television? Most Americans seem to think so. One survey found that seventy-five percent of Americans felt that television had "too much sexually explicit material." Moreover, eighty-six percent believed that television had contributed to "a decline in values."[112] Channel surfing through the television reveals plots celebrating premarital sex, adultery, and even homosexuality.

The Extent of the Problem

Sexual promiscuity in the media appears to be at an all-time high. A study of adolescents (ages twelve to seventeen) showed that watching sex on TV influences teens to have sex. Youths were more likely to initiate intercourse as well as other sexual activities.[113]

A study by the Parents Television Council found that prime time network television is more violent than ever before. In addition, they found that this increasing violence is also of a sexual nature. They found that

---

[112] National Family Values: A Survey of Adults conducted by Voter/Consumer Research (Bethesda, MD, 1994).

[113] Rebecca Collins, et. al., "Watching Sex on Television Predicts Adolescent Initiation of Sexual Behavior," *Pediatrics*, Vol. 114 (3), September 2004.

portrayals of violence are up seventy-five percent since 1998.[114]

The study also provided expert commentary by Deborah Fisher, Ph.D. She states that children, on average, will be exposed to a thousand murders, rapes, and assaults per year through television. She goes on to warn that early exposure to television violence has "consistently emerged as a significant predictor of later aggression."[115]

A previous study by the Parents Television Council compared the changes in sex, language, and violence between decades. The special report entitled *What a Difference a Decade Makes* found many shocking things.[116]

First, on a per-hour basis, sexual material more than tripled in the last decade. For example, while references to homosexuality were once rare, now they are mainstream. Second, the study found that foul language increased five-fold in just a decade. They also found that the intensity of violent incidents significantly increased.

These studies provide the best quantifiable measure of what has been taking place on television. No longer can defenders of television say that TV is "not that bad." The evidence is in, and television is more offensive than ever.

Christians should not be surprised by these findings. Sex and violence have always been part of the human condition because of our sin nature (Romans 3:23), but modern families are exposed to a level of sex and

---

[114] Kristen Fyfe, "More Violence, More Sex, More Troubled Kids," *Culture and Media Institute*, 11 January 2007, www.cultureandmediainstitute.org.

[115] Ibid.

[116] Parents Television Council, Special Report: What a Difference a Decade Makes, 30 March 2000, www.parentstv.org.

violence that is unprecedented. Obviously, this will have a detrimental effect. The Bible teaches that "as a man thinks in his heart, so is he" (Proverbs 23:7, KJV). What we see and hear affects our actions. And while this is true for adults, it is especially true for children.

Television's Impact on Behavior

What is the impact of watching television on subsequent behavior? There are abundant studies which document that what you see, hear, and read does affect your perception of the world and your behavior.

The American Academy of Pediatrics in 2000 issued a "Joint Statement on the Impact of Entertainment Violence on Children." They cited over one thousand studies, including reports from the Surgeon General's office and the National Institute of Mental Health. They say that these studies "point overwhelmingly to a causal connection between media violence and aggressive behavior in some children."[117]

In 1992, the American Psychological Association concluded that forty years of research on the link between TV violence and real-life violence has been ignored, stating that "the 'scientific debate is over' and calling for federal policy to protect society."[118]

A 1995 poll of children ten to sixteen years of age showed that children recognize that "what they see on television encourages them to take part in sexual activity too soon, to show disrespect for their parents, [and] to lie and to engage in aggressive behavior." More than

---

[117] Joint Statement on the Impact of Entertainment Violence on Children, *American Academy of Pediatrics*, 26 July 2000.

[118] David Grossman, "What the Surgeon General Found; As Early as 1972, the Link Was Clear Between Violent TV and Movies and Violent Youths," *Los Angeles Times*, 21 October 1999, B-11.

two-thirds said they are influenced by television; seventy-seven percent said TV shows too much sex before marriage, and sixty-two percent said sex on television and in movies influences their peers to have sexual relations when they are too young. Two-thirds also cited certain programs featuring dysfunctional families as encouraging disrespect toward parents.

The report reminds us that television sets the baseline standard for the entire entertainment industry. Most homes (ninety-eight percent) have a television set. And according to recent statistics, that TV in the average household is on more than eight hours each day.[119]

By contrast, other forms of entertainment (such as movies, DVDs, CDs) must be sought out and purchased. Television is universally available, and thus has the most profound effect on our culture.

As Christians we need to be aware of the impact television has on us and our families. The studies show us that sex and violence on TV can affect us in subtle yet profound ways. We can no longer ignore the growing body of data that suggests that televised imagery does affect our perceptions and behaviors. So we should be concerned about the impact television (as well as other forms of media) has on our neighbors and our society as a whole.

Sex on Television

Most Americans believe there is too much sex on television. A survey conducted in 1994 found that seventy-five percent of Americans felt that television had "too much sexually explicit material." Moreover, eighty-

---

[119] "Average home has more TVs than people," *USA Today*, 21 September 2006, www.usatoday.com/life/television/news/2006-09-21-homes-tv_x.htm

six percent believed that television had contributed to "a decline in values."[120] As we documented earlier, sexual promiscuity on television is at an all-time high.

Many studies on pornography illustrate the dangerous effects of sex, especially when linked with violence.[121] Neil Malamuth and Edward Donnerstein document the volatile impact of sex and violence in the media. They say, "There can be relatively long-term, anti-social effects of movies that portray sexual violence as having positive consequences."[122]

In a message given by Donnerstein, he concluded with this warning and observation: "If you take normal males and expose them to graphic violence against women in R-rated films, the research doesn't show that they'll commit acts of violence against women. It doesn't say they will go out and commit rape. But it does demonstrate that they become less sensitized to violence against women, they have less sympathy for rape victims, and their perceptions and attitudes and values about violence change."[123]

It is important to remember that these studies are applicable not just to hard-core pornography. Many of the studies used films that are readily shown on television (especially cable television) any night of the week. And many of the movies shown today in theaters are much more explicit than those shown just a few years ago.

---

[120] National Family Values: A Survey of Adults conducted by Voter/Consumer Research (Bethesda, MD, 1994).

[121] Kerby Anderson, "The Pornography Plague," Probe Ministries, 1997, www.probe.org/pornography/.

[122] Neil Malamuth and Edward Donnerstein, *Pornography and Sexual Aggression* (New York: Academic, 1984).

[123] Edward Donnerstein, "What the Experts Say," a forum at the Industry-wide Leadership Conference on Violence in Television Programming, 2 August 1993, in *National Council for Families and Television Report*, 9.

Social commentator Irving Kristol asked this question in a *Wall Street Journal* column: "Can anyone really believe that soft porn in our Hollywood movies, hard porn in our cable movies and violent porn in our 'rap' music is without effect? Here the average, overall impact is quite discernible to the naked eye. And at the margin, the effects, in terms most notably of illegitimacy and rape, are shockingly visible."[124]

Christians must be careful that sexual images on television don't conform us to the world (Rom. 12:2). Instead we should use discernment. Philippians 4:8 says, "Finally, brothers, whatever is true, whatever is noble, whatever is right, whatever is pure, whatever is lovely, whatever is admirable, if anything is excellent or praiseworthy, think about such things."

Sex on television is at an all-time high, so we should be even more careful to screen what we and our families see. Christians should be concerned about the images we see on television.

Violence on Television

Children's greatest exposure to violence comes from television. TV shows, movies edited for television, and video games expose young children to a level of violence unimaginable just a few years ago. The American Psychological Association says the average child watches eight thousand televised murders and one hundred thousand acts of violence before finishing elementary school.[125] That number more than doubles by the time he or she reaches age eighteen.

---

[124] Irving Kristol, "Sex, Violence and Videotape," *Wall Street Journal*, 31 May 1994.

[125] John Johnston, "Kids: Growing Up Scared," *Cincinnati Enquirer*, March 20, 1994, p. E01.

At a very young age, children are seeing a level of violence and mayhem that in the past may have been seen only by a few police officers and military personnel. TV brings hitting, kicking, stabbings, shootings, and dismemberment right into homes on a daily basis.

The impact on behavior is predictable. Two prominent Surgeon General reports in the last two decades link violence on television and aggressive behavior in children and teenagers. In addition, the National Institute of Mental Health issued a ninety-four page report, *Television and Behavior: Ten Years of Scientific Progress and Implications for the Eighties.* They found "overwhelming" scientific evidence that "excessive" violence on television spills over into the playground and the streets.[126] In one five-year study of 732 children, "several kinds of aggression, conflicts with parents, fighting and delinquency, were all positively correlated with the total amount of television viewing."[127]

Long-term studies are even more disturbing. University of Illinois psychologist Leonard Eron studied children at age eight and then again at eighteen. He found that television habits established at the age of eight influenced aggressive behavior throughout childhood and adolescent years. The more violent the programs preferred by boys in the third grade, the more aggressive their behavior, both at that time and ten years later. He therefore concluded that "the effect of television violence on aggression is cumulative."[128]

---

[126] Cited in "Warning from Washington," *Time*, 17 May 1982, 77.

[127] James Mann, "What Is TV Doing to America?" *U.S. News and World Report*, 2 August 1982, 27.

[128] Leo Bogart, "Warning: The Surgeon General Has Determined that TV Violence Is Moderately Dangerous to Your Child's Mental Health," *Public Opinion* (Winter, 1972-73): 504.

112

Twenty years later Eron and Rowell Huesmann found the pattern continued. He and his researchers found that children who watched significant amounts of TV violence at the age of eight were consistently more likely to commit violent crimes or engage in child or spouse abuse at thirty.[129] They concluded that: "heavy exposure to televised violence is one of the causes of aggressive behavior, crime and violence in society. Television violence affects youngsters of all ages, of both genders, at all socioeconomic levels and all levels of intelligence."[130]

Violent images on television affect children in adverse ways and Christians should be concerned about the impact.

Biblical Perspective

Television is such a part of our lives that we often are unaware of its subtle and insidious influence. Nearly every home has a television set, so we tend to take it for granted and are often oblivious to its influence.

I've had many people tell me that they watch television, and that it has no impact at all on their worldview or behavior. However the Bible teaches that "as a man thinks in his heart, so is he" (Proverbs 23:7). What we view and what we think about affects our actions. And there is abundant psychological evidence that television viewing affects our worldview.

George Gerbner and Larry Gross, working at the Annenberg School of Communications in the 1970s, found that heavy television viewers live in a scary world. "We have found that people who watch a lot of TV see

---

129 Peter Plagen, "Violence in Our Culture," *Newsweek*, 1 April 1991, 51.

130 Ibid.

the real world as more dangerous and frightening than those who watch very little. Heavy viewers are less trustful of their fellow citizens, and more fearful of the real world."[131] Heavy viewers also tended to overestimate their likelihood of being involved in a violent crime. They defined heavy viewers as those adults who watch an average of four or more hours of television a day. Approximately one-third of all American adults fit that category.

If this is true of adults, imagine how television violence affects children's perceptions of the world. Gerbner and Gross say, "Imagine spending six hours a day at the local movie house when you were twelve years old. No parent would have permitted it. Yet, in our sample of children, nearly half of the twelve-year-olds watch an average of six or more hours of television per day." This would mean that a large portion of young people fit into the category of heavy viewers. Television profoundly shapes their view of the world. Gerbner and Gross therefore conclude: "If adults can be so accepting of the reality of television, imagine its effect on children. By the time the average American child reaches public school, he has already spent several years in an electronic nursery school."[132]

Television viewing affects both adults and children in subtle ways. We must not ignore the growing body of data that suggests that televised imagery does affect our perceptions and behaviors. Our worldview and our subsequent actions are affected by what we see on television. Christians, therefore, must be careful not to let television conform us to the world (Romans 12:2), but instead should develop a Christian worldview.

---

[131] George Gerbner and Larry Gross, "The Scary World of TV's Heavy Viewer," *Psychology Today*, April 1976.

[132] Ibid.

CHAPTER 11 New Media and Society

Kerby Anderson

How is the new media affecting the way we think and the way we interact with others in society? I want to look at the impact the Internet, social networks, and portable media devices are having on our world.

Rachel Marsden doesn't think it is positive. Writing in *The Wall Street Journal* she says:

> Spare me the stories of your "genius" tech-savvy child who can name every country on Google Earth, or how, because of your iPhone, BlackBerry and three cell phones, you juggle 20 tasks at once and never miss any business—even at 4 a.m., because you sleep with your portable devices. Does anyone care that technology is destroying social graces and turning people into rude jerks?[133]

She isn't the first to notice that the new technology and new mobile devices are changing the way we interact with others. And, as we will discuss later, they apparently are also changing the way we think, affecting everything from creativity to concentration.

Rachel Marsden wonders, "When did it become acceptable for technological interaction to supersede in-person communication?" I have news for her. It happened long before cell phones were invented. When I was a graduate student at Yale University, I noticed something odd about my academic advisor. Whenever

---

[133] Rachel Marsden, "Technology and the New Me Generation," *The Wall Street Journal*, 30 December 2009.

the phone would ring, he felt he had to answer it. He could be advising me or we could be deep in the midst of a discussion of a research project. But if the phone rang, he stopped the conversation and answered the phone, staying on the phone until that conversation was over. I began to think that the only way I could ever have a sustained conversation with him would be to call him on the phone.

Of course, mobile devices make it even easier to ignore face-to-face interaction. Now the world revolves around the person who has instant access to others using these devices. Rebecca Hagelin says that narcissism has crept into our world. In 2006, *Time* magazine voted "You" as the "Person of the Year." So much of media and advertising today is about indulging your fantasies.

Rebecca Hagelin is concerned about the impact this is having on our children. "Young people spend hours every day updating their Facebook pages, post and e-mail countless pictures of themselves, and plug their ears with music to create a self-indulgent existence shut-off from everyone around them."[134]

While some of the impact is positive, much more should concern us and cause us to change our behavior.

The Internet and the Way You Think

Can the Internet change how you think? That was a question columnist Suzanne Fields asked recently.[135] If you go to Edge.org, you will notice that the question they pose for this year is slightly different. It is, "How is the Internet changing the way you think?" They pose this

[134] Rebecca Hagelin, "Narcissism and Your Family," 15 February 2010, www.townhall.com/hagelin.

[135] Suzanne Fields, "Can the Internet Change How You Think?" 15 January 2010, www.townhall.com/fields.

provocative question because of the impact of computer chips, digitized information, and virtual reality on the way we think and how we receive information in this "collective high-tech electronic ecosystem for the delivery of information."

I have also been wondering about the impact of the Internet and the new media on our thinking. Unlike Suzanne Fields, I wasn't wondering *if* the Internet was changing our thinking but *how* it is already changing the way we think. There were two reasons why I have been thinking about this.

First, look at the younger generation being raised on the Internet. If you haven't noticed, they think and communicate differently from previous generations. I have done radio programs and read articles about the millennial generation. They do think differently, and a large part of that is due to the Internet.

A second reason for my interest in this topic is an *Atlantic* article by Nicholas Carr entitled "Is Google Making Us Stupid?" He says, "Over the past few years I've had an uncomfortable sense that someone, or something, has been tinkering with my brain, remapping the neural circuitry, reprogramming the memory."[136]

It's not that he believes his mind is going, but he notices that he isn't thinking the way he used to think and he isn't concentrating like he used to concentrate. "Immersing myself in a book or a lengthy article used to be easy. My mind would get caught up in the narrative or the turns of the argument, and I'd spend hours strolling through long stretches of prose. That's rarely the case anymore. Now my concentration often starts to drift after two or three pages."

---

136 Nicholas Carr, "Is Google Making Us Stupid?" *Atlantic*, July/August 2008.

He believes this comes from using the Internet and searching the web with Google. And he gives not only his story, but he also gives many anecdotes and as well as some research to back up his perspective.

For example, a developmental psychologist at Tufts University explains, "We are not only what we read. We are how we read." The style of reading on the Internet puts "efficiency" and "immediacy" above other factors. Put simply, it has changed the way we read and acquire information.

Now you might say that would only be true for the younger generation. Older people are set in their ways. The Internet could not possibly change the way the brains of older people download information. Not true. The 100 billion neurons inside our skulls can break connections and form others. A neuroscientist at George Mason University says, "The brain has the ability to reprogram itself on the fly, altering the way it functions."[137]

The Internet does appear to be altering the way we read and think, but more research is needed to confirm if this true. If so, parents and educators need to take note of what is happening in our cyberworld.

BlackBerries, Twitter, and Concentration

Have portable media devices altered our ability to concentrate? That certainly seems to be the case. Nearly all of us have noticed that people with a BlackBerry sometimes seem distracted. And after they answer an e-mail, they seem to spend a few minutes trying to recollect their thoughts before they had the interruption.

[137] Ibid.

An article in *Newsweek* magazine documents what many of us have always suspected: there are two major drawbacks to these devices.[138] The first is distraction overload. A study at the University of Illinois found that if an interruption takes place at a natural breakpoint, then the mental disruption is less. If it came at a less opportune time, the user experienced the "where was I?" brain lock.

A second problem is what is called "continuous partial attention." People who use mobile devices (like a BlackBerry or an iPhone) often use their devices while they should be paying attention to something else. Psychologists tell us that we really aren't multitasking, but rather engage in rapid-fire switching of attention among tasks. It is inevitable they are going to miss key information if part of their focus is on their BlackBerry.

But another hidden drawback associated is less creativity. Turning on a mobile device or a cell phone when you are "doing nothing" replaces what we used to do in the days before these devices were invented. Back then, we called it "daydreaming."

That is when the brain often connects unrelated facts and thoughts. You have probably had some of your most creative ideas while shaving, putting on makeup, or driving. That is when your brain can be creative. Checking e-mail reduces daydreaming.

We also can see how new technology affects the way we process information and react to it emotionally. The headline of one article asked this question: Can Twitter make you amoral?[139] Research was done at the

---

138 Sharon Begley, "Will the BlackBerry Sink the Presidency?" *Newsweek*, 16 February 2009.

139 "Can Twitter Make You Amoral? Rapid-fire Media May Confuse Your Moral Compass," 14 April 2010, www.in.com.

Brain and Creativity Institute of the University of Southern California to see the impact of social networks like Twitter.

What the researchers found was that human beings can sort information very quickly. And they can respond in fractions of seconds to signs of physical pain in others. But other emotions (like admiration and compassion) take much longer to register. In fact, they found that lasting compassion in a relationship to psychological suffering requires a level of persistent, emotional attention.

So how does that relate to a technology like Twitter? The researchers found that there was a significant emotional cost of heavy reliance on a rapid stream of news snippets obtained through television, online feeds, or social networks such as Twitter. One researcher put it this way: "If things are happening too fast, you may not even fully experience emotions about other people's psychological states and that would have implications for your morality."

The point of these studies is that media does have an impact. A wise and discerning Christian will consider the impact and limit its negative effects.

Social Networks

Social networks such as Facebook and MySpace create an interconnected web of friends and family. People who study these networks are beginning to understand the impact they are having on us.

At a social networking site, you find someone and ask to be his or her friend. Once you are accepted, you become a member of their network, and they become a member of your network. This opens to door to finding and making additional friends. The ability to extend your circle of friends is one of the many benefits of social networking.

One concern about social networking is that it, like most of the new media, increases distraction and fragmentation of thought. The quotes, stories, jokes, and video clips come at an increased rate. A concentrated conversation with one person is difficult. Look over the shoulder of someone in a social networking site who has lots of friends. Content quickly scrolls downward, and it feels like you are at a party where lots of people are all talking at once.

Also these networks tend to shorten our time of concentration. Steven Kotler makes this case in his *Psychology Today* blog, "How Twitter Makes You Stupid."[140] He once asked the author of the best-selling book why he called it the "8 Minute Meditation." The author told him that eight minutes was the length of time of an average segment of television. He reasoned that "most of us already know exactly how to pay attention for eight minutes."

Steven Kotler argues that Twitter is reducing the time of concentration to a few dozen words. He thinks that constantly using Twitter will tune "the brain to reading and comprehending information 140 characters at a time." He predicts "that if you take a Twitter-addicted teen and give them a reading comprehension test, their comprehension levels will plunge once they pass the 140 [character] mark." I am sure someone is already testing that hypothesis. Soon we should know the results.

Social networks do help us keep track of people who do not live near us, and that's a plus. But we are

---

[140] Steven Kotler, "How Twitter Makes You Stupid," Psychology Today, 15 May, 2009, www.psychologytoday.com/blog/the-playing-field/200905/how-twitter-makes-you-stupid.

kidding ourselves if we believe that social networks are the same thing as true community. Shane Hipps, writing in *Flickering Pixels*, says this about virtual communities: "It's virtual—but it ain't community."

Social networks also have a great deal of power to influence us. Sociologists Nicholas Christakis and James Fowler document this in their new book, *Connected: The Surprising Power of Our Social Networks and How They Shape Our Lives.* They believe that happiness is contagious and so is obesity and quitting smoking. We are not only influenced by our friends, but are even influenced by our friend's friends. They say the world is governed by what they call "three degrees of separation."

Addiction is another concern. Years ago, counselors discovered Internet addiction. Now they are starting to talk about Facebook addiction. Lots of youth and adults spend too much time in front of a computer. Social networks are wonderful tools, but wisdom and discernment are necessary in order to use them correctly.

Media Addiction

The Barna Group does lots of surveys, and that has led George Barna to conclude that "media exposure has become America's most widespread and serious addiction."[141] I have always been hesitant to label our high levels of media exposure an addiction. We seem to have an addiction label for every behavior. But George Barna makes a convincing case.

Addiction changes our brains by altering the chemical balance and flow within the brain and by even altering the structure of the brain. According to the

---

[141] George Barna, "Media Addiction," 25 January 2010, www.barna.org.

American Psychiatry Association, we can legitimately call something an addiction when certain symptoms manifest themselves.

For example, addictions change our brain structure, altering emotions, motivations, and memory capacity. Addictions cause withdrawal symptoms when exposure to the addictive item is eliminated. Addictions cause the people to abandon or reduce their involvement in normal and healthy activities.

Certainly, media can be positive in terms of education and relaxation. But most media content, Barna argues, "winds up serving the lowest common denominator because that's where the largest audience" is to be found.

There is a generational trend. The builder generation did not grow up with media and never became accustomed to it. The boomer generation embraced media, and the following generations expanded it use in ways unthinkable a few decades ago.

If we were truly serious about controlling the media input in our lives and our children's lives, we would see examples of parents putting boundaries on media exposure. We see nothing of the sort. Expenditures on personal media, in-home media, and mobile media continue to increase.

It is not that parents don't understand the dangers. Barna reports that three-quarters of parents say that exposure of their children to inappropriate media content are one of their top concerns. But they continue to buy their kids the media tools and continue to allow them to be exposed to inappropriate content.

By the time a young person reaches age 21, he or she will have been exposed to more than 250,000 acts of violence through TV, movies, and video games. He or she will have listened to thousands of hours of music with questionable lyrical content.

Most parents know that much of what their children see or hear isn't wholesome

This may be one of the biggest challenges for society in general and even the church in particular. Most parents recognize the danger of the media storm in which they and their children live. But that are unwilling to take the necessary steps to set boundaries or end their media addiction.

Biblical Principles

There is a crucial need for Christians to evaluate the impact of media in their lives. We need to develop discernment and pass those biblical principles to our children and grandchildren.

The new media represents an even greater threat and can easily conform us to the world (Rom. 12:2). Media is a powerful tool to conform us to a secular worldview and thus take us captive (Col. 2:8) to the false philosophies of the world.

Christians should strive to apply the following two passages to their lives as they seek discernment concerning the media. The first is Philippians 4:8. "Finally, brothers, whatever is true, whatever is noble, whatever is right, whatever is pure, whatever is lovely, whatever is admirable—if anything is excellent or praiseworthy—think about such things."

The second is Colossians 3:2–5. "Set your minds on things above, not on earthly things. For you died, and your life is now hidden with Christ in God. When Christ, who is your life, appears, then you also will appear with him in glory. Put to death, therefore, whatever belongs to your earthly nature: sexual immorality, impurity, lust, evil desires and greed, which is idolatry."

CHAPTER 12 Media and Discernment

Kerby Anderson

We live in the midst of a media storm. Every day we are confronted by more media messages than a previous generation could even imagine.

Media Exposure

For example, more homes have TV sets (98 percent) than have indoor plumbing. In the average home the television set is on for more than six hours a day. Children spend more time watching television than in any other activity except sleep.[142] Nearly half of elementary school children and 60 percent of adolescents have television sets in their bedrooms.[143]

But that is just the beginning of the media exposure we encounter. The *Journal of the American Medical Association*estimates that the average teenager listens to 10,500 hours of music during their teen years.[144] Families are watching more movies than every before since they can now watch them on cable and satellite and rent or buy movies.

---

[142] Huston and Wright, University of Kansas, "Television and Socialization of Young Children."

[143] E.H. Woodard and N. Gridina, *Media in the Home: The Fifth Annual Survey of Parents and Children 2000* (Philadelphia, PA: The Annenberg Public Policy Center of the University of Pennsylvania, 2000).

[144] Elizabeth F. Brown and William R. Hendee, "Adolescents and Their Music: Insights Into the Health of Adolescents," *The Journal of the American Medical Association* 262 (September 22-29, 1989): 1659.

The amount of media exposure continues to increase every year. Recent studies of media usage reveal that people spend more than double the time with media than they think they do. This amounts to nearly twelve hours a day total. And because of media multitasking, summing all media use by medium results in a staggering fifteen hours per day.[145]

Student use of the Internet has been increasing to all-time levels. A study done at the University of Massachusetts at Amherst found the following:[146]

- Nearly 90 percent of the students access the Internet every day.

- Students spent over ten hours per week using IM (instant messaging).

- Those same students spent over twenty-eight hours per week on the Internet.

- Nearly three-fourths spent more time online than they intended.

In addition to concerns about the quantity of media input are even greater concerns about the quality of media input. For example, the average child will witness over 200,000 acts of violence on television, including 16,000 murders before he or she is 18 years old. And consider that the average child views 30,000 commercials each year.

A study of adolescents (ages 12-17) showed that watching sex on TV influences teens to have sex. Youths

---

145 Robert A. Papper, et. al., "Middletown Media Studies," *International Digital Media & Arts Association Journal*, Vol. 1, No. 1, Spring 2004, 5.

146 Gary D. Malaney, "Student Internet Use at UMass Amherst," *Student Affairs Online*, Vol. 5, No. 1, Jan. 2004.

were more likely to initiate intercourse as well as other sexual activities.[147]

Over 1000 studies (including reports from the Surgeon General's office and the National Institute of Mental Health) "point overwhelmingly to a causal connection between media violence and aggressive behavior in some children."[148]

To put it simply, we are awash in media exposure, and there is a critical need for Christians to exercise discernment. Never has a generation been so tempted to conform to this world (Rom. 12:1-2) because of the growing influence of the proliferating forms of media.

Biblical Discernment

Although the Bible does not provide specific instructions about media (you can't find a verse dealing with television, computers, or DVDs), it nevertheless provides broad principles concerning discernment.

For example, the apostle Paul in 2 Timothy 2:22 instructs us to "Flee from youthful lusts." We should stay away from anything (including media) that inflames our lust. Paul also goes on to say that in addition to fleeing from these things, we should also "pursue righteousness, faith, love and peace." We should replace negative influences in our life with those things which are positive.

Paul says in Colossians 3:8, "But now you must rid yourselves of all such things as these: anger, rage, malice, slander, and filthy language from your lips." Now, does that mean you could never read something that has

---

[147] Rebecca Collins, et. al., "Watching Sex on Television Predicts Adolescent Initiation of Sexual Behavior," *Pediatrics*, Vol. 114 (3), September 2004.

[148] Joint Statement on the Impact of Entertainment Violence on Children, American Academy of Pediatrics , 26 July 2000.

anger or rage or slander in it? No. After all, the Bible has stories of people who manifest those traits in their lives.

What Paul is saying is that we need to rid ourselves of such things. If the input into our lives (such as through media) manifests these traits, then a wise and discerning Christian would re-evaluate what is an influence in his or her life.

Paul tells us in Philippians 4:8, "Finally, brothers, whatever is true, whatever is noble, whatever is right, whatever is pure, whatever is lovely, whatever is admirable—if anything is excellent or praiseworthy— think about such things." We should focus on what is positive and helpful to our Christian walk.

We are also admonished in Romans 13:13 to "behave decently as in the daytime, not in orgies and drunkenness, not in sexual immorality and debauchery, not in dissension and jealousy."

As Christians, we should develop discernment in our lives. We can do this in three ways: stop, listen, and look. Stop what you are doing long enough to evaluate the media exposure in your life. Most of us just allow media to wash over us every day without considering the impact it is having on us.

Second, we should listen. That is, we should give attention to what is being said. Is it true or false? And what is the message various media are bringing into our lives?

Finally, we should look. We need to look at the consequences of media in our lives. We should rid ourselves of influences that are negative and think on those things that are positive.

Worldview of the News Media

Of all the forms of media, the news media have become a primary shaper of our perspective on the world. Also, the rules of journalism have changed in the last few decades. It used to be assumed that reporters or broadcasters would attempt to look at events through the eyes of the average reader or viewer. It was also assumed that they would not use their positions in the media to influence the thinking of the nation but merely to report objectively the facts of an event. Things have changed dramatically in the news business.

The fact that people in the media are out of step with the American people should be a self-evident statement. But for anyone who does not believe it, there is abundant empirical evidence to support it.

Probably the best-known research on media bias was first published in the early 1980s by professors Robert Lichter and Stanley Rothman. Their research, published in the journal *Public Opinion*[149] and later collected in the book *The Media Elite*,[150] demonstrated that reporters and broadcasters in the prestige media differ in significant ways from their audiences.

They surveyed 240 editors and reporters of the media elite—*New York Times*, *Washington Post*, *Time*, *Newsweek*, ABC, NBC, and CBS. Their research confirmed what many suspected for a long time: the media elite are liberal, secular, and humanistic.

People have always complained about the liberal bias in the media. But what was so surprising is how liberal members of the media actually were. When asked

---

[149] S. Robert Lichter and Stanley Rothman, "Media and Business Elites," *Public Opinion*, (October-November 1981): 42-46.

[150] S. Robert Lichter, Stanley Rothman, and Linda S. Lichter, *The Media Elite* (New York: Adler and Adler, 1986).

to describe their own political persuasion, 54 percent of the media elite described themselves as left of center. Only 19 percent described themselves as conservative. When asked who they voted for in presidential elections, more than 80 percent of them always voted for the Democratic candidate.

Media personnel are also very secular in their outlook. The survey found that 86 percent of the media elite seldom or never attend religious services. In fact, 50 percent of them have no religious affiliation at all.

This bias is especially evident when the secular press tries to cover religious events or religious issues. Most of them do not attend church, nor do they even know people who do. Instead, they live in a secularized world and therefore tend to underestimate the significance of religious values in American lives and to paint anyone with Christian convictions as a "fundamentalist."

Finally, they also found that the news media was humanistic in their outlook on social issues. Over 90 percent of the media elite support a woman's so-called "right to abortion" while only 24 percent agreed or strongly agreed that "homosexuality is wrong."

For a time, members of the media elite argued against these studies. They suggested that the statistical sample was too small. But when Robert Lichter began to enumerate the 240 members of the news media interviewed, that tactic was quickly set aside. Others tried to argue that, though the media might be liberal, secular, and humanistic, it did not affect the way the press covered the news. Later studies by a variety of media watchdogs began to erode the acceptance of that view.

A second significant study on media bias was a 1996 survey conducted by the Freedom Forum and the Roper

Center.[151] Their survey of 139 Washington bureau chiefs and congressional correspondents showed a decided preference for liberal candidates and causes.

The journalists were asked for whom they voted in the 1992 election. The results were these: 89 percent said Bill Clinton, 7 percent George Bush, 2 percent Ross Perot. But in the election, 43 percent of Americans voted for Clinton and 37 percent voted for Bush.

Another question they were asked was, "What is your current political affiliation?" Fifty percent said they were Democrats, 4 percent Republicans. In answer to the question, "How do you characterize your political orientation?" 61 percent said they were liberal or moderately liberal, and 9 percent were conservative or moderately conservative.

The reporters were also asked about their attitudes toward their jobs. They said they see their coverage of news events as a mission. No less than 92 percent agreed with the statement, "Our role is to educate the public." And 62 percent agreed with the statement, "Our role is sometimes to suggest potential solutions to social problems."

A more recent survey by the Pew Research Center further confirms the liberal bias in the media. They interviewed 547 media professionals (print, TV, and radio) and asked them to identify their political perspective. They found that 34 percent were liberal and only 7 percent were conservative. This compares to 20 percent of Americans who identify themselves as liberal and 33 percent who define themselves as conservative.[152]

---

[151] S. Robert Lichter, "Consistently Liberal: But Does It Matter?" *Media Critic* (Summer 1996): 26-39.

[152] "Survey: Liberals dominate news outlets: Far higher number in press than in general population," *WorldNetDaily*, 24 May 2004.

It is also worth questioning whether a majority of media professionals who labeled themselves as moderate in the survey really deserve that label. John Leo, writing for *U.S. News and World Report*, says that it has been his experience "that liberal journalists tend to think of themselves as representing the mainstream, so in these self-identification polls, moderate usually translates to liberal. On the few social questions asked in the survey, most of the moderates sounded fairly liberal."[153]

Once again, we see the need for Christians to exercise discernment in their consumption of media.

Biblical Principles and Application

Christians must address the influence of the media in society. It can be a dangerous influence that can conform us to the world (Rom. 12:2). Therefore we should do all we can to protect against its influence and to use the media for good.

Christians should strive to apply the following two passages to their lives as they seek discernment concerning the media: Philippians 4:8, which we quoted above, and Colossians 3:2–5: "Set your minds on things above, not on earthly things. For you died, and your life is now hidden with Christ in God. When Christ, who is your life, appears, then you also will appear with him in glory. Put to death, therefore, whatever belongs to your earthly nature: sexual immorality, impurity, lust, evil desires and greed, which is idolatry."

Here are some suggestions for action.

First, control the quantity and quality of media input. Parents should set down guidelines and help select television programs at the start of the week and watch only those. Parents should also set down guidelines for

---

153 John Leo, "Liberal media? I'm shocked!" *U.S. News and World Report*, 7 June 2004, 12.

movies, music, and other forms of media. Families should also evaluate the location of their television set so that it is not so easy to just sit and watch TV for long hours.

Second, watch TV with children. One way to encourage discussion with children is to watch television with them. The plots and actions of the programs provides a natural context for discussion. The discussion could focus on how cartoon characters or TV characters could solve their problems without resorting to violence. What are the consequences of violence? TV often ignores the consequences. What are the consequences of promiscuous sex in real life?

Third, set a good example. Parents should not be guilty to saying one thing and doing another. Neither adults nor children should spend long periods of time in front of a video display (television, video game, computer). Parents can teach their children by example that there are better ways to spend time.

Fourth, work to establish broadcaster guidelines. No TV or movie producer wants to unilaterally disarm all the actors on their screens for fear that viewers will watch other programs and movies. Yet many of these TV and movie producers would like to tone down the violence, even though they do not want to be the first to do so. National standards would be able to achieve what individuals would not do by themselves in a competitive market.

Fifth, make your opinions known. Writing letters to programs, networks, and advertisers can make a difference over time. A single letter may not make a difference, but large numbers of letters can even change editorial policy. Consider joining with other like-minded people in seeking to make a difference in the media.

While the media has a tremendous potential for good, it can also have some very negative effects. Christians need wisdom and discernment to utilize the positive aspects of media and to guard against its negative effects.

Appendix: How and Why We Should Biblically Analyze Songs

Sarah Withers

Numerous scientific studies have revealed that music is linked to relieving pain/stress, releasing endorphins, aiding coordination, increasing concentration, expanding memory, improving language skills, and lowering blood pressure, just to list a few.[154] Unfortunately, not all genres of music offer these benefits, so it would be quite misleading to say that critically analyzing songs can act as a remedy for migraines—however convenient and persuasive that claim might be!

While I may not be able to claim health advantages, powerful benefits can be gleaned for us and others by being aware and graciously critical of songs. I hope that I can provide how and why we should biblically analyze songs and challenge you to be a more thoughtful and gracious critical consumer of all types of music.

How Do We Biblically Analyze a Song?

The most obvious first step to biblically analyzing a song is to actively listen to the lyrics and even watch the music video. It helps me focus and understand if I pull up the lyrics and read along as I listen. While I listen, I think about how the song makes me feel, what the song got right or wrong in its worldview, what I appreciate about the song, and any questions about possible meanings and

---

[154] Another article that was particularly helpful was from http://www.emedexpert.com/tips/music.shtml. However, if you just search "benefits to music" (or the like) and you will be overwhelmed by how many articles develop all the unique benefits to music.

interpretations. I also think about if or how I can relate to the song's message. Have I ever experienced, desired, or seen something similar to the song's message? If the answer is no, then maybe I could think about how seeing the songwriter's perspective could help me relate and communicate with someone with very different desires and experiences than my own.

Ultimately, we biblically critique a song by shining the light of the biblical truths on it. No secular song gets everything right for the obvious reason that the gospel is not present. For some songs all that is missing is an explicit reference to the gospel, while other songs directly conflict with the gospel. Yet, for even the more difficult songs, Christians can understand the song's message for the glory of God.

For example, Lana Del Rey's song "Born to Die"[155] provides the message that we should enjoy life because when we die there is nothing left for us. For those in Christ, that song is radically wrong about our purpose and destiny.

However, for those who are outside of Christ, that song paints a rather apt picture of their bleak destiny.[156] So yes, the song is very dark and upsetting, yet when I hear that song I can mourn for those outside of Christ and praise God that the lyrics of that song are not true for me. In that way, that song can incite worship and foster resolve to reach out to unbelievers-something Del Rey probably would never consider possible! That is the

---

[155] The video includes sexual content, brief drug use, and a violent image at the end.

[156] I should note however, that the song seems to hold the message of mere extinction at death. As Christians, we believe that souls are immortal which means even the non-believer persists. For those outside of Christ, they will experience death as eternal wrath and destruction. See John 3:36, Roman 6:23, Matthew 25:46, 2 Thessalonians 1:9, and Revelation 21:8.

transformative power of the gospel, the greatest good news.

However, there are songs that Christians should avoid. Songs that are overly sexualized or demonic in nature may be too difficult to redeem.[157] Also some people are more affected by music than others. If you are not able to redeem the song by countering it with life-giving truths from Scripture and the song continues to bring you down, then you should not listen to it. Christians should pray for wisdom and guidance to know when to listen and engage and when to turn it off.[158]

Why Should We Care?

Since music is so integrated into our daily lives, many of us are consumers of music whether we are intentional about it or not. The American Academy of Pediatrics (in 1996) found that 14- to 16-year-olds listened to an overage of 40 hours of music per week.[159] For a more conservative number, the Radio and Internet Newsletter reported that students "spend an average of 7

---

[157] To address briefly the pushback on the idea that we can or should "redeem culture": The confusion rests in the nuanced difference in meaning of the word "redeemed." I use the word "redeemed" in this context to mean something closer to transformed by truth, not redeemed in the sense God has redeemed believers. Yes, Scriptures never call us to "redeem culture" but God does call us to let the light of truth shine. By engaging culture with the truth of Scriptures, Christians can make aspects of culture honoring to God, thus in that sense redeeming them. For example, pornography falls under the category of "unredeemable," meaning that there is no way someone could make pornography honoring to God. However, with different aspects of culture this task is possible and I think should be encouraged.

[158] Hebrews 5:14.

[159] Impact of Music Lyrics and Music Videos on Children and Youth, http://www.public.asu.edu/~dbodman/candv/aap_musiclyrics_videos.pdf

138

hours and 38 minutes a day consuming media, 2 hours 19 minutes of which is spent listening to music."[160]

While these studies focus on teens and adolescents, it is fair to say that adults also listen to a fair amount of music, whether it is through headphones at work or the radio in the car. When it comes down to it, music is very much part of our everyday life. For some it can be avoided, but by most, it is accepted and greatly enjoyed.

Musical lyrics are also sticky. It never ceases to amaze me how I can still easily sing along to songs from my childhood the second the second it plays. Yet, when discussing my project of biblically analyzing popular music, a common response is that people often do not listen to the lyrics, but rather just enjoy the melody and beat. The AAP (1996) reported that "in one study 30% of teenagers knew the lyrics to their favorite songs," which would seem to affirm that initial claim.

With those intuitions and findings, it would be easy to undermine this project as interesting but unimportant. However, the same AAP (2009) article cited the Knobloch-Westerwick *et al.* study that "although young listeners might not understand all the details in lyrics, they recognize enough to obtain a general idea of the message they bring."

Moreover, the fact that we do remember song lyrics well after we have stopped listening to them shows that we are aware of the words even if we are not actively thinking about the message. In many respects we have become passive consumers of information and

---

[160] RAIN cited the Kaiser Family Foundation study for these statistics, http://textpattern.kurthanson.com/articles/870/rain-125-kaiser-study-finds-youth-spend-over-2-hours-a-day-listening-to-music. The report also broke down how the kids and teens were listening to the music, finding that on average per day they listen to 41 minutes of music on their IPod and similar devices, 32 minutes of music on computers (iTunes and Internet radio), and 32 minutes listening to the radio.

entertainment, especially when it comes to music. It is in light of this passivity that we should strive to be active listeners.

Every song with words carries a message, although some are more obvious and dangerous than others. For example, current artists such as Macklemore, Hozier, Lana Del Rey, and Lady Gaga proclaim more explicit messages and agendas in their songs-something as Christians we should be aware of and ready to critique. The AAP (1996) claimed that "awareness of, and sensitivity to, the potential impact of music lyrics by consumers, the media, and the music industry is crucial."

Although the rate and impact of the consumption of songs can be debated, there are still benefits of being aware of and engaging with our culture through songs.

What Are the Benefits?

Well, there are three main benefits to biblically analyzing songs. First, we refine our ability to enjoy music. For many this will be very counterintuitive. People I have talked with have feared that if they are too critical of the music's message, then they will no longer be able to enjoy it. I will agree, there are some songs that might be ruined by listening critically to the lyrics. However, Christians should likely avoid listening to those songs anyway.

Even with songs we don't like, we can still enjoy them for their musicality and benefit from some insights, however hard to find. The vast majority of songs are redeemable even though they may counter the gospel. Where God provides the songwriter with common grace insights, there is an opportunity to redeem the song. Remember Lana Del Rey's song; I am still able to enjoy her powerful use of a darker sound and message, but I am also reminded of the hope I have in the gospel.

If we get to a point where we become cynical and antagonistic towards our music culture, we should remember that God gave us music and culture as a gift. The Psalms are examples of a great variety of songs that were written to offer the expression of truth about God, humanity, and our world. The obvious difference is that the Psalms are God-breathed and inspired—yet there are often truths that can be gleaned even from secular and popular songs. After all, we are all made in God's image and bear His music-loving traits.

Another benefit of analyzing songs is the ability to learn about our culture and the people influenced by it. Regardless of whether the lyrics are true, they are believed to be true by the songwriter and often by people in our culture. Part of the appeal of songs is that they are relatable. Relatability makes the song powerful and influential.

We can gain invaluable insight into the thoughts of our culture and younger generations through the lyrics of songs. Many songs provide commentary on our culture's view of alcohol consumption, drug use, violence, relationships, sexuality, freedom, and self-worth. By learning what the songs say about such topics, we can be better equipped to understand where people are coming from.

The final benefit, which naturally flows from the previous one, is being able to relate and engage with our culture. By engaging with themes in songs, we are ultimately practicing how to engage with people. I was talking with a group of high school students about one of Macklemore's songs called "Starting Over" which is about his relapse as an alcoholic. The song is marked with shame, a deep sense of failure, and loss of identity. Before listening to the song, I encouraged them to listen to the lyrics as if a person was talking with them. With that perspective, students would be less likely to immediately judge him as a failure, and instead would be more likely to empathize and relate, as we are all failures and slaves to sin outside of Christ.

By being aware of songs, we can better engage the lies of our culture and counter them with the truths of Scripture.[161] The AAP (1996 & 2009), encourages parents to "become media-literate" which means, "watching television with their children and teenagers, discussing the content with them, and initiating the process of selective viewing at an early age." Later in the article, the authors even suggest that parents should look up the lyrics and become familiar with them. Even if you are not a parent, as Christians one way we can help correct lies of our culture is through conversations about popular music.

Paul wrote in 2 Corinthians 4:6, "For God, who said, 'Let light shine out of darkness,' has shone in our hearts to give the light of the knowledge of the glory of God in the face of Jesus Christ." It is our hope and joy that we have been redeemed and my prayer that Christians will show others the light of Christ.

So, the goal of analyzing songs from a Christian perspective is not merely an academic exercise that challenges critical thought, but to move us to action. Peter claimed that Christians were saved so "that you may proclaim the excellencies of Him who called you out of darkness into His marvelous light" (1 Peter 2:9). Ultimately, we should be encouraged to talk, relate, empathize, and love others. Through songs we can help others to "See to it that no one takes you captive by philosophy and empty deceit, according to human tradition, according to the elemental spirits of the world, and not according to Christ" (Colossians 2:8).

---

[161] See Ephesians 6:17-20 and 2 Corinthians 10:1-6.

142

Bibliography

Anderson, Kerby. *Christian Ethics in Plain Language.* Nashville, TN: Thomas Nelson, 2005.

Godawa, Brian. *Hollywood Worldviews: Watching Films with Wisdom & Discernment.* Downers Grove, IL: InterVarsity Press, 2009.

Henry, Carl F. H. *Christian Personal Ethics* (Chapter 18). Grand Rapids, Mich.: Baker, 1957.

Lawhead, Stephen R. *Turn Back the Night: A Christian Response to Popular Culture.* Westchester: Crossway, 1985.

Lewis, C. S. *The Abolition of Man.* New York: Macmillan, 1947.

Lichter, Robert, Stanley Rothman, and Linda S. Lichter, *The Media Elite.* New York: Adler and Adler, 1986.

Medved, Michael. *Hollywood vs. America: Popular Culture and the War on Traditional Values.* New York: Harper Collins/Zondervan, 1992.

Myers, Kenneth A. *All God's Children and Blue Suede Shoes: Christians & Popular Culture.* Westchester: Crossway, 1989.

Newport, John. *Theology and Contemporary Art Forms.* Waco, Tex.: Word, 1971.

Ryken, Leland, ed. *The Christian Imagination: Essays on Literature and the Arts.* Grand Rapids, Mich.: Baker, 1981.

Schaeffer, Francis A. *Art and the Bible.* Downers Grove, Ill.: InterVarsity, 1973.

Schultze, Quentin J., et al. *Dancing in the Dark: Youth, Popular Culture, and the Electronic Media*. Grand Rapids, Mich.: Eerdmans, 1991.

Schultze, Quentin J. *Redeeming Television*. Downers Grove, Ill.: InterVarsity, 1992.

144

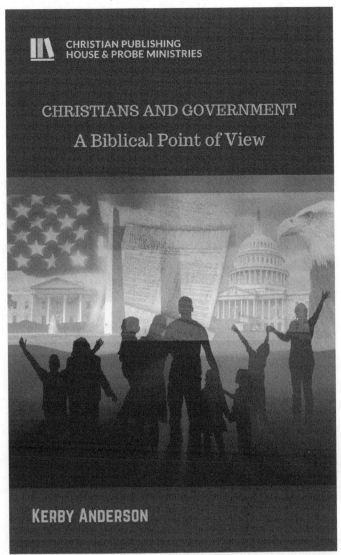

**CHRISTIAN PUBLISHING
HOUSE & PROBE MINISTRIES**

CHRISTIANS AND GOVERNMENT

A Biblical Point of View

KERBY ANDERSON

CHRISTIAN PUBLISHING
HOUSE & PROBE MINISTRIES

CHRISTIANS AND ECONOMICS
A Biblical Point of View

KERBY ANDERSON

For the love of money is a root of all
sorts of evil.—1 Tim. 6:10, NASB.

CHRISTIAN PUBLISHING
HOUSE & PROBE MINISTRIES

TECHNOLOGY AND SOCIAL TRENDS

A Biblical Point of View

KERBY ANDERSON

Like Israel in the days of David, 'are we ones who have an understanding of the times, to know what we as Christians ought to do?'—1 Chron 12:32.

147

99754378R00087

Made in the USA
Columbia, SC
13 July 2018